THE KNACK

STAFF

Editors
Martin Preston
Richard Chapman

Art Editors
Maggi Howells
Jonathan Alden

Deputy Editor
Martin Derrick

Projects Editor
Andrew Kemp

Senior Sub Editor
Brenda Marshall

Sub Editors
Barry Milton
Trevor Morris
Gregor Ferguson
Tom Hibbert
John Ward

Designers
Lee Thomas
Shirin Patel
Christina Fraser
Chris Legee

Technical Consultant
George Smith

Technical Artist
Antonio Toma

Editorial Secretary
Sue Ashby

Staff Photographer
Ray Duns

Projects
Alan Cornish
Clive Padget

Picture Research
Anne Lyons

Production Executive
Robert Paulley

Production Controller
Patrick Holloway

Editorial Assistant
Jill Wiley

Cover Design
Jim Bamber

Production Secretary
Linda Mifsud

Reference Edition published 1984

©MCMLXXX MCMLXXXI MCMLXXXII
Marshall Cavendish Limited
58 Old Compton Street
London W1V 5PA

Printed and bound in Italy by L.E.G.O. S.p.a.

ISBN 0 85685 999 0 (Set)
ISBN 0 85685 988 5 (Vol 14)

The Knack
1. Dwellings—Remodeling—Amateurs'
manuals
I. Chapman, Richard
643'.7   TH4816

ISBN 0-85685-999-0

THE KNACK

THE ILLUSTRATED ENCYCLOPEDIA OF HOME IMPROVEMENTS

Volume 14

Marshall Cavendish · London & New York

Contents

Repairing garage doors

● **Types of garage door** ● **Problems associated with side-hung doors** ● **How to tackle warped doors** ● **Refurbishing door joints** ● **Bracing a sagging door** ● **Replacing parts of wooden doors** ● **Repairing part of a rotten frame**

Garage doors are larger, heavier, more exposed, and—because they open outwards—easier to damage than any other exterior or interior doors around the house. Some repair techniques for interior and exterior doors have already been described (see pages 705 to 709), and these are equally valid for garage doors too. But garage doors have their own peculiar problems, many of which you can easily tackle yourself in order to save money, protect your home, and preserve its appearance.

Garage doors fall into two distinct categories: the traditional ledged and boarded or framed, side-hung wooden doors; and the wide range of metal or wooden doors which slide, fold, or can be lifted into position by a series of guides or tracks. Wooden side-hung doors are still by far the most common, even though they are more likely to need repair or replacement than metal ones (fig. B).

Side-hung doors

Side-hung garage doors are attractive and can easily be made to match your house, but they must be carefully maintained if they are to remain serviceable. Garage openings are usually about 2.1m wide by 2m high and the sheer weight of the doors can cause serious joint sag—making them difficult to open and close, and generally unsightly. Slight warping and twisting can often be cured with the doors in situ by forcing them against the twist. Do this with cramps, against a heavy object or a fixed board to provide the necessary leverage.

With more serious cases, remove the doors and cramp them against the twist on a flat surface. This alone may cure the problem, especially if you soak the timber first to make it more pliable. But if you still have no luck, fit some form of bracing (figs C and F) while the doors are cramped.

In the worst cases, you must draw the door frame square with sash cramps and reinforce the existing mortise and tenon joints with adhesive or extra screws. For a more professional job, it is better to dismantle the offending frame completely and refurbish the joints. When you come to reassemble it, drill, glue and insert strengthening dowels to supplement the existing tenons.

Whenever you remove a door, lay it flat and take out any glazed panels before starting work. You must also remove any old bolts which no longer

Garage doors suffer from all the problems that normally affect doors, but their weight and exposed position means that rot around the hinges can make them sag badly

Chris Fairclough

1 *If the door stile is as rotten as this, you may have to replace part of it. This can be done with the door in place if necessary*

2 *When you have determined the extent of the rot, saw through the stile above the rotten section from each side of the door*

3 *When you have made the saw cuts, chisel away the rotten timber from around the tenons on the rail. Be careful not to damage them*

support the door effectively, or which impede your efforts to straighten it, and this can be a troublesome process—especially if the bolts are rusted.

If you cannot loosen coachbolts with penetrating oil, try cutting a slot in the bolt head with a hacksaw so that you can use a large screwdriver. If this fails, drill into the head of the bolt with a twist-drill as near the size of the bolt shank as possible. Flatten the bolt head with a rough file so that the drill bit does not slip and damage the wood, then slowly drill through the head until it drops away.

When you have squared up the door

B. Below left: *A typical arrangement of a side-hung wooden door, timber door frame, and the slightly raised garage floor*
C. Below right: *One way of bracing a sagging door—the steel bar is fixed to the door with coachbolts at as many points as possible*

so that its diagonal dimensions are identical, drill out any splintered or rotten wood from the old bolt holes and fill them with a hard-setting epoxy or resin filler. When this has set, re-drill the holes so that you can screw new bolts into the door.

Bracing

In most cases the repairs described above will be enough to keep the doors intact. But because garage doors are much heavier than other doors, it is well worthwhile fitting additional strutting to prevent problems from recurring. One way of doing this is to attach a metal bracing bar diagonally across the back of the door. Use a mild steel bar about 6mm thick and between 25 and 50mm wide, and run this from the top end of the stile on the hinge side to the bottom end of the stile on the shutting side. Make sure that the bar does not extend beyond the edges of the door, then secure it

with a number of 8mm coach bolts at intervals along its length (fig. C).

Some ironmongers and steel stockists will supply a bar cut and drilled to your specifications, although it may be less trouble to buy a plain bar and make the holes yourself.

In this case use a centre punch to locate the position of the bolt holes. Drill the pilot holes with a 2.5–3mm twist drill, then drill the final bolt holes. If you are using a power drill, use it on a low speed setting and lubricate the bit with oil as you drill

As an alternative you can use a bracing (or straining) wire to support the door. Like the steel brace, this runs from the top corner of the hinge stile to the bottom corner of the opposite stile. A screw-tightening device (similar to the bottle screws used to tighten the mast stays on sailing craft) lies diagonally on the door; when tightened, this lifts the bottom of the closing stile and keeps it

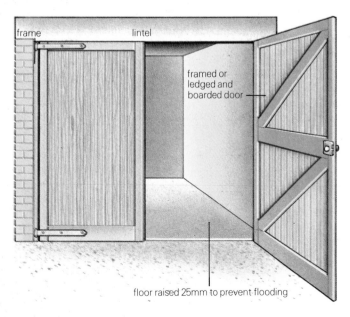

frame

lintel

framed or ledged and boarded door

floor raised 25mm to prevent flooding

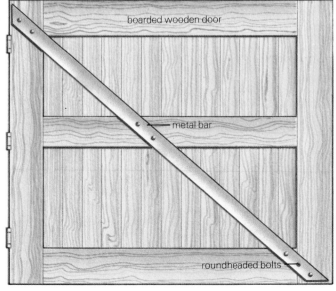

boarded wooden door

metal bar

roundheaded bolts

Bernard Fallon

4 *Cramp the new section of timber in place, make sure that it is correctly aligned, and then mark the position of the scarf joint*

5 *Use a mortise gauge to transfer the dimensions of the tenons to the new stile, and a mortise chisel to cut the mortises*

6 *If the door has a rebated shutting stile, you will have to duplicate this on the replacement section using a rebate plane*

7 *Use a hammer and a block of scrap timber to knock the new piece into place, then check the fit. Be careful not to damage the tenons*

8 *When you are satisfied that the new section fits correctly you can remove it, glue the joints, and screw it into position*

9 *When you have reinforced the mortise and tenon joint with a screw or dowel, you can paint the wood with preservative and primer*

Chris Fairclough

clear of the floor when the door is re-hung (fig. F).

To prevent the door warping, cut notches in the corners of the stiles so that you can run the wire down both sides. Use staples to hold the wire in place (fig. F). You can then re-hang the door and adjust the tensioner until the door hangs properly.

Although you can use ordinary fencing wire and a tensioning device available from a hardware store, a ship's chandler will stock wire cable and a bottle screw adjuster that will do an equally good job. And bottle screws have the additional advantage that, being designed for a salt-water environment, they tend to resist corrosion more effectively.

A less unsightly preventive measure is to fit a wheel castor to the bottom of the shutting stile. This will take the weight of the door when it is opened and closed, at the same time lifting the bottom edge off the ground.

Remove the door to fit the castor, and screw the bracket to the rail rather than to the comparatively weak end grain of the stile. If possible, choose a spring-loaded castor that will ride over the unevenness of your drive.

Door rot

One common cause of door sag is wet rot in the wood, and the weight of a garage door tends both to exaggerate and accelerate the effects. Bad cases of rot and door sag entail dismantling the affected door and replacing rotten sections in their entirety.

Early signs of rot are blistering and bubbling in the paintwork. Determine to what extent it has taken hold by sticking the blade of a penknife into the suspect areas until you reach sound timber.

The most commonly affected areas are the bottom rail, the ends of the stiles, and the edges of glazed panels. In the latter case the cause is normally rainwater running down the glass and behind the beading or rebated edge of the panel.

Having cut out and patched the rotted section, bed the glass in an ample amount of putty smoothed level

with the beaded edge (see pages 593 to 596) to prevent the problem re-curring. Efficient puttying is particularly important in cases where the glass is patterned or reinforced with wire mesh because water can seep through the joints with the beading.

If the rot extends beyond more than one of the joints of the stile, you will have to replace the stile completely.

Start by removing the door and placing it on a flat surface or two trestles. Drill out any dowels or mortise wedges in the joints, using a wooden block to protect the edges of the timber. Then knock the stile outwards from the rails with a hammer so that the tenons on the rails separate from their mortises. Use a softwood block to prevent the hammer blows from damaging the stile itself.

Work your way slowly from joint to joint until the stile is released, then measure up the tenons on the rails and cut corresponding mortises in the new stile. Clean down the surfaces of all the joints in the new stile and knot and prime them before applying the

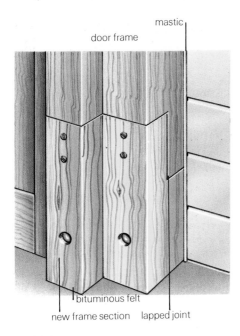

D. *Door frame repairs need to be strong enough to stand up to the weight of the door, and adequately protected against damp and rot*

door frame
mastic
bituminous felt
new frame section
lapped joint

adhesive and sash cramps (see pages 111 to 114). Use a waterproof adhesive —urea or resorcinol formaldehyde.

Alternatively, you can saw through the stile immediately adjacent to the joints and chisel away the rotten wood from around the joint area before replacing it.

If only one joint on the stile has rotted, you can cut out the rotted section and replace it with a new joint. To do this, cut through the stile immediately above the rotted section and chisel or prise off the damaged wood, being careful to leave the tenon on the adjoining rail undamaged.

Cut a new section 75mm longer than the piece you have removed, and finish the end of the replacement piece in the way shown in fig. E. Cut a joint in the stile above the damaged section to correspond with the replacement section. This creates a strong and durable scarf joint which can be secured with screws and dowels. Cut mortises in the other end of the replacement piece to accept the tenons in the stile.

Again, knot and prime all the surfaces of the new wood, including the joints, and glue and cramp the new wood into position before fastening the scarf joint with screws. For

10 *If you want to replace part of a door frame, the first stage is to remove the door and also the door stop, if it is of the planted type*

additional strength secure the mortise and tenon joint between stile and rail with a dowel and insert wedges against the tenons (fig. E). Plane and smooth all the edges, then prime and paint them.

Often the tenons on the lower rail suffer from rot. If both ends are damaged replace the entire rail, but if only one end is damaged you can replace it in the manner described above, or construct a 'false tenon' that is jointed into the rail and held

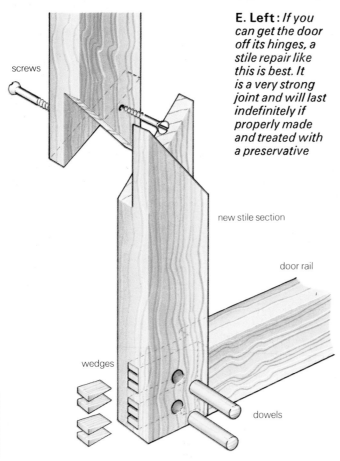

door stile
screws
new stile section
door rail
wedges
dowels

E. Left: *If you can get the door off its hinges, a stile repair like this is best. It is a very strong joint and will last indefinitely if properly made and treated with a preservative*

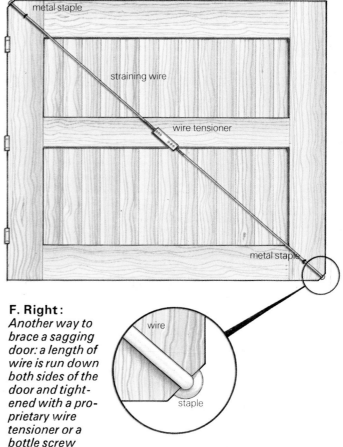

metal staple
straining wire
wire tensioner
metal staple
wire
staple

F. Right: *Another way to brace a sagging door: a length of wire is run down both sides of the door and tightened with a proprietary wire tensioner or a bottle screw*

Bernard Fallon

11 *When you have cut off the rotten part of the frame, use a tenon saw or a chisel to cut out a lapped joint in the frame member*

12 *Cut out a similar lapped joint in the replacement section of timber, making sure that it exactly matches the one on the frame*

13 *Whether you are screwing or bolting the new piece to the wall, drill holes for the wallplugs or masonry bolts into the brickwork*

14 *Before screwing and bolting the new piece of timber into place, treat it with a waterproof sealer at the back and on its foot*

15 *Fit the door hinge into position in the new frame section and check its strength before you treat it with preservative and paint*

with glued dowels.

Tongued-and-grooved boards on traditional ledged and boarded doors often shrink, leaving exposed gaps between them. This is not only unsightly but also allows water to enter and rot the timber. The effect can be most damaging where the panels shrink away from the stiles to form a crack in the paintwork—allowing water to enter and rot the stiles. The most frequent cause is insufficient seasoning and, in acute cases, the best thing to do is to replace the boarding, cramping the new panels tightly together as you do so.

Treat minor cases by scraping off the cracked paintwork down to clean timber with a shave hook and then forcing a flexible epoxy filler into the gaps. These fillers are elastic enough to take up considerable movement in the boards, but they will not adhere properly unless the timber is completely free of paint. Once the filler has gone 'off', rub down any rough edges and repaint the door.

Repairing a rotten frame
Frame damage generally occurs at the bases of the uprights, which are exposed and more likely to absorb water from the ground. Determine the extent of the damage as above by probing the timber with a penknife.

Cut out the damaged section well past the rot and chisel a lapped joint at the base of the timber which remains, as shown in fig. D. Then cut a replacement piece of timber to match the frame and form a lapped joint at the top to mate with the one you have just cut. As door frames can be bought in standard sizes, to match most existing frames, you should have no trouble finding a compatible piece of timber.

Drill screw holes in the replacement section, both to secure the lapped

joint and to allow for the timber to be screwed or bolted to the adjoining masonry. Then locate it in position and mark the positions of the holes in the masonry with a hammer and a long masonry nail or drill bit.

Remove the replacement section, drill out the holes in the wall with a masonry bit, and insert wallplugs to take No. 12 woodscrews. Alternatively use expanding wall bolts. Then prime the back of the replacement section and glue a piece of bituminous felt to the foot to prevent the rot from recurring.

Before gluing and screwing the new section to the original frame, check that it aligns correctly and if necessary insert blocks of wood behind it to take up any unevenness in the wall. Finally, screw or bolt the new section to the wall, screw and glue the lapped joint, and knot, prime and paint the timber before replacing the door. Seal the entire frame with a non-hardening mastic at the point where it meets the masonry: this will help prevent moisture attacking the joint from behind.

Alternatives to side-hinged doors
Not all wooden doors are side-hinged: there are designs on the market for folding, sliding, and up-and-over doors made in timber, and they all suffer from problems similar to those described above. Many others, however, are manufactured in galvanized steel, aluminium, or glass fibre. All of them, including the wooden doors, run in guides or a variety of lifting mechanisms so that they open into an unobtrusive position. Their most frequent problem, therefore, apart from those problems shared with wooden doors, is that the tracking or lifting systems may fall out of adjustment as the door frames start to rot, or if the garage itself starts to settle with old age. Procedures for repairing them will obviously vary from one design to another, but most manufacturers supply full fitting and constructional details which include maintenance and adjustment instructions. You can refer to these if you encounter any of the problems with the doors, frames, or tracks mentioned above.

Chris Fairclough

The modern look

To some people the modern look seems stark and bare, but if it is done well it is a stunning style of decoration. Simple, uncluttered lines, neutral or bold colours and plain or geometric patterned fabrics are the key points

Below: *The soft, neutral colours of the walls and carpet plus a simple glass coffee table between the leather seating combine to achieve a relaxing, uncluttered look in this modern-style living room*

Among the many different styles of furnishing and decorating a home, one of the easiest and most labour-saving schemes is the modern look. Although many people might find the modern style stark and bare, its furniture and furnishings are easy to clean and the neutral colours often used are relaxing to the eye.

The modern style calls for a spacious look with no unnecessary furniture—each piece being carefully chosen to fulfill a particular purpose. The overall effect should be one of uncluttered, streamlined efficiency with simple shapes and no unnecessary ornament. There should be a predominance of straight lines and flat surfaces, although some curves—perhaps a moulded plastic chair—may be introduced for dramatic effect.

Colour schemes are usually light, with plenty of white. Simple, emulsion-painted walls in neutral shades such as white, cream and grey will achieve the right look. Pattern should be added with extreme caution.

On the whole, the modern style favours geometric designs rather than florals and tends to use boldly pronounced pattern concentrated into one area, rather than having it scattered around the room.

Generally speaking, patterned wall papers are not in keeping with the modern style of decoration. However, it is possible to introduce texture by using a fabric wallcovering such as hessian or wool.

In a large room it is possible to make one wall a feature of the room by covering it—or even part of it—in a natural material such as wood cladding, cork, or brick. In older houses you may be able to strip away plaster to reveal attractive brickwork underneath. This can either be cleaned off to its natural colouring or painted in white or cream.

Floorcoverings too should be in pale tones wherever practical and if you want a patterned carpet, it is best to choose a neat, all-over geometric design. Again, you can introduce texture by using plain twist piles or

Elizabeth Whiting

Jessica Strang

Rivista Deli Arremento

Above: *A quarry tile platform, covered with window seat cushions, creates an unusual, but practical feature. The geometric print of the cushions has been chosen to tone perfectly with the curtains*
Left: *Furniture, in different shades of green, is set off well by white walls which are decorated simply with large, square picture frames*

long shaggy piles. A cork or wood floor also provides a good background for a modern setting.

Another good alternative where the floorboards are in fairly good condition is to sand and seal them. You can then add a modern Scandinavian wool rya rug, or a flat weave kelim or oriental rug with a geometric design to introduce warmth and colour.

In a dining room or hallway where the floor is likely to receive a lot of wear, and collect more dirt, plain vinyl tiles or sheeting is probably the best choice.

A spacious effect, which is such an important aspect of the modern style, can often be heightened with a clever use of mirrors—on walls, doors or celings. They can give an impression of doubling the space within a room.

Another, more radical, alternative for achieving a spacious effect is to remove all, or part, of a wall to open up your house. A popular modern arrangement is to combine kitchen, dining room and living room into one big living area. However, it is best to take expert advice before making any structural alterations.

Modern-style furniture

For furniture and furnishings the modern style can quite happily mix both natural and man-made materials and is not averse to imitations, so long as they are very skilful. For example, a plastic laminate imitation of marble, or a PVC leather look is perfectly acceptable providing the effect is realistic.

Otherwise, choose natural materials such as wool, cotton, leather, cork, stone and all kinds of wood so long as the natural grain is not concealed by heavy polish or stains. Man-made materials might include metals such as steel, often with a shiny chrome finish, aluminium, glass and all kinds of plastics moulded into exciting and unusual shapes.

Ideally, furniture should be low and streamlined. Modern seating has abandoned the three-piece suite in favour of compact units grouped in an L or U shape to suit the room. Modern look furniture is often flexible, and sometimes serves a dual role—for instance seating doubling as a bed; tables and beds comprising storage space; adjustable shelves and furniture units which can combine into different sizes and arrangements.

Solid foam sofas and chairs which can convert to a bed in seconds are inexpensive and ideal for a modern setting. Otherwise, look for comfortable yet stylish seating in textured coverings like tweedy or knubbly

Jessica Strang

Below: *To avoid a stark look in this dining room, different tones of beige have been combined to create a warm, welcoming atmosphere*

Above: *A bedroom which would be suitable for a teenager needing plenty of storage space. Bold colours are an important feature of the room*

fabrics, smooth weaves in wool, corduroy or linen union—or for a more expensive look, in leather. Avoid shiny materials like velvets or figured brocades and choose plain rather than patterned fabrics unless they are of a geometric design. Again, wherever practical, choose pale colours such as oatmeal or peat.

Small, low tables with wood, marble, glass or perspex tops in wood or steel frames are ideal for books, magazines and the occasional TV snack meal. Table and chair legs are often replaced by pedestals to give a more elegant look that is also easier to clean.

Streamlined storage

Storage furniture should be as unobtrusive as possible and it is a good idea to concentrate all the storage requirements of a room on to one wall.

Wall storage units can be bought or made to your own design to fit along side each other and fill up any given space. Various compartments and drawers provide space for anything from cutlery, china and glassware to television, hi-fi and records.

Sometimes it is possible to give older more ornate pieces of furniture a modern feel simply by painting them to merge in with their background.

Bedroom fittings

In the bedroom, too, streamlined fittings have taken over from the more

Left: *A room which makes the most of natural daylight through the windows and the roof. A plant and two pictures prove quite sufficient adornment*

conventional wardrobe, dressing table and chest of drawers. Now, even the beds are low and streamlined and often incorporate storage drawers below. Some types even have elaborate headboards incorporating all manner of modern electronics, including a telephone, hi-fi system, television and

radio, door entry phone and so on.

Again, furniture may be finished in medium to pale colour woods such as teak, pine, ash or beech, though more sophisticated, luxurious, modern pieces may be made of richly-figured rosewood. Otherwise a simple finish of white melamine, plain and unadorned,

is perfectly suitable in most cases.

Windows are an important part of the modern style and elaborate curtain treatments which may block off natural light from the room should be avoided at all costs.

Multi-paned windows look very attractive for some styles, but for a modern look they should be replaced by a single sheet of glass. Pelmets are not in keeping with a modern scheme —unless they are specially designed to suit the room and windows—and curtains are best left loose without elaborate swags or tie backs. Use plain white track and simple gathered or pinch pleated heading for curtains.

Choose only bold, striking, geometric or abstract designs for bedroom curtains or stick to plain fabrics which can be trimmed with a decorative border or a single row of braid, mitred at the corners for a tailored effect.

The modern trend is to leave windows unscreened during the day, though plain, heavy nets or 'sheers' or

loosely woven linens or acrylics can be used to provide a degree of privacy. To screen the room by night, either draw the curtain across the window or use roller blinds, featuring a bold, modern design. On a large window it is often better to have two or three individual roller blinds than one large, cumbersome one. Venetian blinds and vertical blinds, particularly in white or silver, also suit the modern style.

Lighting is sophisticated and subtle and should be designed to enhance the room, emphasizing the effect of the lighting rather than the fittings themselves. Spotlights mounted on tracks for greater flexibility are popular, both for general lighting and for highlighting pictures or objects.

Remember that the modern style is clean and uncluttered, and decorative extras should be kept to a minimum. It is better to have one large, impressive picture or print than a cluster of small ones. Similarly, avoid collections of ornaments, using instead just one or two striking pieces of china, treasured porcelain, or sculpture.

Greenery always fits well into modern interiors—particularly large, leafy plants which create a dramatic effect in the room. Cheese plants, aspidistras and rubber plants are the perennial favourites, but smaller green and variegated plants can look equally good when highlighting furniture.

Left: *A modern look kitchen which exemplifies the principle of clean, simple lines—giving a feeling of space and organization*
Below: *In this modern bedroom a platform has been covered with plain carpeting—a design which looks best in a good-sized room*

Siematic UK Ltd

Elizabeth Whiting

Reinforcing concrete

- **Reinforcing slab foundations using steel mesh**
- **Strengthening concrete lintels** ● **Building a brick soldier arch** ● **House wall reinforcement** ● **Points to bear in mind when using reinforced steel inserts**

Concrete is a robust material which will support heavy loads and withstand great pressures. Yet if it is subjected to any unnatural loadings, stresses eventually develop which cause the material to split and crack. The tensile strength of concrete—its ability to resist such pressures—is greatly increased by inserting reinforcements in the form of either rolled steel bars or galvanized wall ties.

Using reinforcements to strengthen concrete is a technique which can be used in a whole variety of building projects around the home. As well as solid concrete structures—such as slab foundations for buildings, lintels and driveways—they are often used in brick and block laying.

A. Below: *Reinforcing steel comes in a large variety of shapes and sizes. It ranges from steel mesh— used to strengthen slab foundations—to expanded metal and light steel ties or extrusions for brick and blockwork*

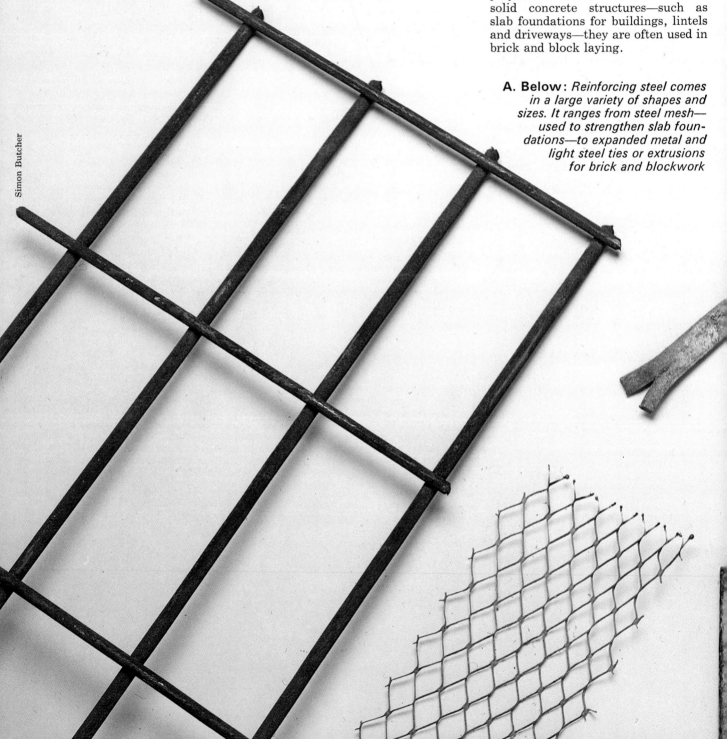

Simon Butcher

Reinforced slab foundations

Perhaps the most common use of reinforced concrete is in foundation work. Although many floors are built without reinforcement, inserting steel mesh into the concrete guarantees a stronger and more durable finish.

Steel bars or twisted wire, formed into square or oblong shaped mesh, is the best type of reinforcement for concrete slabs. Such material is available in rolls or sheets 2.4m wide and 4.8m long. Both the main and cross wires are the same size, and vary in diameter from 3mm to 10mm.

For most domestic constructions, such as driveways, patios and outhouses, 3mm or 5mm mesh is most suitable. Before you order it, measure the area to be covered carefully, remembering that a gap of about 50mm should be left between the outside of the mesh and the edge of the concrete slab.

Mesh can be ordered ready cut into sections about 2m² so that they fit neatly into standard-sized concreting bays. But if you have a large area to cover and need to fit the mesh around obstacles such as drains and awkward corners, it is easier to order one or more complete sheets and cut them to size on site. Use a heavy duty wire cutter (bolt cutters) for this—a hacksaw will prove incapable of dealing with rolled steel.

To cut costs, or if sheet material is not available, you can make your own mesh using steel bars and heavy duty wire. Lay out a row of bars spaced at 200mm intervals and then another at right-angles over the top of them, also 200mm apart. Wrap a short length of wire around each of the overlaps and tighten it securely with pliers. Once all the bars are attached in this way, the mesh is ready to be positioned.

Once you have laid out the bays ready for concreting (see pages 272 to 277), fix battens of wood half as high as the formwork at intervals of roughly 1m along the inside of the bays. These will support the mesh sheeting above the ground and hold it in position so that it can be completely enveloped by concrete (fig. B).

Pick up the lengths of mesh and lay them across the top of the formwork. Then move systematically around the outside of each bay cutting the mesh to size with the wire cutters so that it drops down on to the battens. At the same time, trim the mesh so that it fits neatly around any obstructions such as drains and house walls.

Once the mesh is set in place, nail further lengths of timber batten on top of the first ones to hold it in position

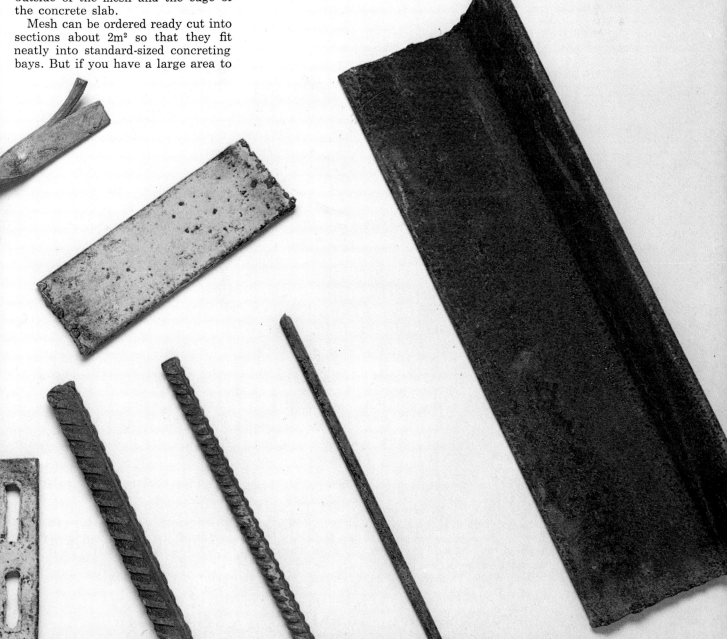

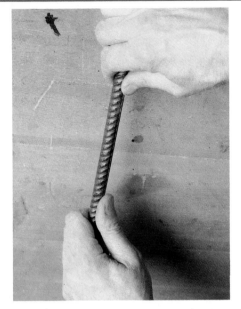

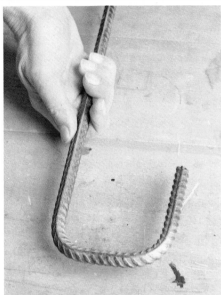

1 To reinforce a concrete lintel, use 12mm rolled steel rods—one rod for every half brick in the thickness of the wall

2 The end of each rod should be bent backwards on itself to strengthen doubly the points bearing the most weight

3 Get the rods bent where you purchase them, or—if you need to make a number of lintels—hire a bending machine

Simon Butcher

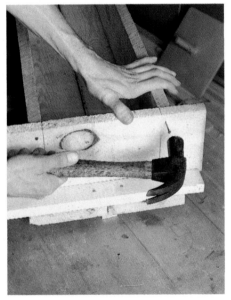

4 Build the formwork for the lintel carefully, taking into account the size of the opening and the width of the wall

5 Nail the sides, ends and bottom of the formwork securely together so that they can bear the weight of the concrete infill

6 Paint the inside of the formwork with oil or a releasing agent. This allows the lintel to separate from the mould once it sets

during concreting. These should be thinner than the lower battens so that they end up at least 50mm below the top edges of the formwork. Unlike the main formwork timbers, they are not knocked away once the concrete has set but remain in place below ground level.

Once you have checked the formwork all round for level with a straightedge and spirit level, the concrete should be mixed and poured. The best mix for foundations and driveways is 1:2:4—one part cement, two parts sand and four parts of 6mm crushed ballast or shingle.

Mix the material thoroughly by hand on a suitable flat surface near the working area. If you have a large slab to lay it may be worth buying or hiring a cement mixer to make the work easier. Alternatively, you may care to order the concrete ready-mixed (see pages 527 to 530). The mix should be fairly wet so that it can flow easily into the formwork and under the steel mesh.

Start from one end of each bay and slowly fill it with concrete until it is just level with, or slightly above, the top of the formwork. Make sure that the concrete is well packed, especially below the mesh, so that air pockets do

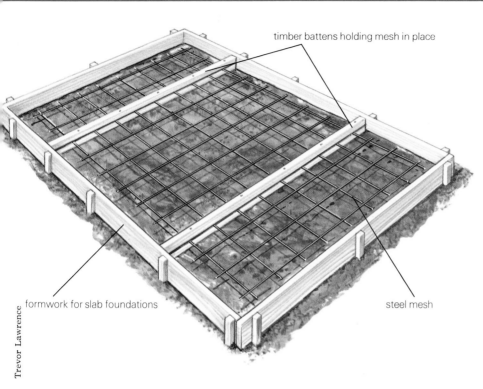

timber battens holding mesh in place

formwork for slab foundations

steel mesh

Trevor Lawrence

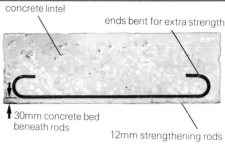

concrete lintel

ends bent for extra strength

30mm concrete bed beneath rods

12mm strengthening rods

C. Above: *Concrete lintels are strengthened by the addition of one or more 12mm diameter rolled steel rods along the base*

B. Above: *Reinforcing a concrete slab with steel mesh greatly increases its strength and long-term durability*

not develop which might lead to subsidence once the slab sets. Use a long, thick batten to push the concrete into the bottom of the formwork or hire a poker-shaped vibrator which is inserted into the drying material to help it settle correctly.

Once all air bubbles are removed, tamp the top of the slab level with the formwork using a heavy length of timber (see pages 272 to 277). Then skim the surface completely flat with a wooden float, or give it a rippled finish by brushing the concrete with a stiff broom or hand brush.

Reinforced lintels
Reinforcement is often added to the concrete or brick lintels which span doorways and windows. This helps the lintel to bear the heavy weight of the wall above it without cracking or splitting, even if slight subsidence occurs. Two or more reinforcing steel bars are introduced into the middle of the lintel during construction and the concrete is then allowed to set around them. However, the technique you use depends on whether you are building a reinforced concrete lintel or constructing a reinforced brick arch:
Concrete lintels: These can either be pre-cast and lifted into place whole or

manufactured in situ above the door or window concerned. Which type you use depends upon both the position for which it is intended and its weight.

If a lintel is longer than 1.8m or wider than 1500mm, it should be cast in situ since it will be too large to lift safely and set in place once it is made. The same applies to lintels which are to go in awkward positions where movement is restricted; the job of building formwork and pouring concrete is likely to prove easier than handling a heavy, pre-cast lintel in such confined spaces.

But if the lintel is to be of reasonable weight and there is plenty of room, always opt for the pre-cast variety. You can cast or buy it before work on the arch takes place, and then have it ready to position without need for interruptions.

Start by calculating the size of the lintel, the amount of reinforcement needed and the bearing on each side of the opening. For any span up to 1.8m a concrete lintel 50mm wide is required with one 12mm strengthening rod for every half-brick in the thickness of the wall to be covered. The bearing on each side of the opening should be equal to one-eighth of the span. For spans above 1.8m wide, consult an architect or building inspector and get him to draw up detailed plans before you start work.

Prepare a framed box of the correct dimensions to cast the lintel (see

pages 1419 to 1424). If the lintel is to be cast in situ, this should be fixed to the brickwork on either side of the arch rather than being cast in a box.

Reinforcing rods for lintels are formed so that each end is bent backwards on itself: this doubly strengthens the lintel ends which bear most of the weight from above. Choose rods which are slightly shorter than the lintel itself so that the ends are covered in concrete on completion.

The rods must be positioned along the *soffit* (base) of the formwork where the greatest tension occurs. So that no bare metal is exposed once they are in place, first mix up a small batch of concrete and lay a thin foundation about 30mm deep along the soffit. Leave this to set a little before carefully positioning the rods on top, an equal distance apart (fig. 8).

Mix up a fresh batch of concrete and shovel it on top of the rods until the whole box is completely filled. To get rid of air pockets and make sure the concrete is well packed, push the end of a batten of wood into the mixture and stir it vigorously from one side to another. The poured concrete should finish flush with the top of the formwork, so level it off with a straight wooden batten run across the top edges of the forming box.

Once the concrete has set—usually at least half a day—knock away the formwork (see pages 1419 to 1424) and leave the lintel for at least another two or three days before lifting it into place or building around it.
Brick lintel: A neat decorative finish can be given to a reinforced concrete lintel by covering it with a *soldier* arch of bricks placed on end or on their sides. To make sure that the arch finishes level with the existing wall, leave enough space for it when you construct the lintel.

Once the lintel is in position and the concrete has set, lay a piece of

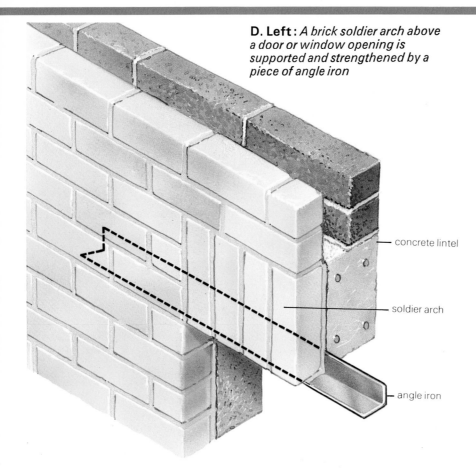

D. Left: *A brick soldier arch above a door or window opening is supported and strengthened by a piece of angle iron*

concrete lintel

soldier arch

angle iron

angle iron wide enough to bear the bricks across the opening in front of it. Make sure that the iron bears on each side of the opening by at least 150mm and that the angle faces inwards so that it will be unseen when the arch is completed (fig. D).

To support the brickwork during construction, a temporary former is built and erected across the opening. The brick arch is then set in place above it and the former removed once the mortar has set. This is covered in the next part of the Masonry course.

Reinforced brickwork

It is often useful to incorporate reinforcements when working with bricks or building blocks. Applications include extension walls, block partitions and free-standing garden walls.

Apart from rolled steel bars, which are occasionally used for vertical reinforcement, nearly all the reinforcements employed in brick or blockwork are inserted on a horizontal

E. Below: *Tramline reinforcement built in above doors and windows*

plane. Used in this way, they can make up for unavoidable breaks in bonding patterns or add strength to corners and changes in section. Single skin block structures are less sturdy than their brick equivalents and reinforcement is nearly always specified by the architect or building inspector (see pages 638 to 643).

Fig. A shows the main reinforcements used; all are mortared into the bedding joints as brick or block laying proceeds. Expanded metal, light mesh, or tramline reinforcement can be used between brick or block courses while twisted metal 'butterfly' ties are generally inserted across the line of the brickwork on a double-thickness or cavity wall.

Strengthening house walls

The walls of most modern houses, extensions and outhouses are built in two layers with a cavity between. The inner wall is usually made of light-weight building blocks while the outer wall consists of bricks. To hold the two leaves together, steel wall ties must be built into the mortar joints between them (see pages 700 to 704).

To strengthen the wall further—particularly if the building is higher than one storey—reinforcement must be added at certain weak points in the structure. These occur at changes of section in a brick wall, particularly above doors and windows (fig. E).

To strengthen these points, two lines of reinforcement should be added—the first one course above the opening and the second three or four courses higher up. The reinforcement should extend 600mm either side of the critical section. And where two openings are in close proximity, the strengthening will bear the stresses better if it is positioned in two lines above and between the openings.

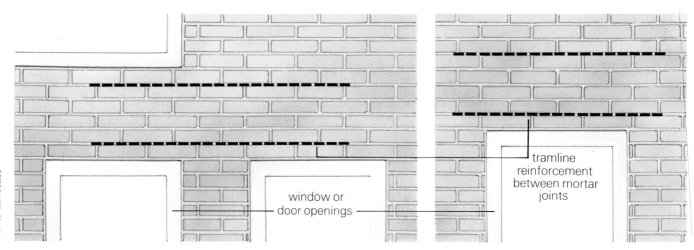

window or door openings

tramline reinforcement between mortar joints

Trevor Lawrence

7 So that no bare metal is exposed once the rods are in place, lay a 30mm deep bed of concrete along the base (soffit) of the formwork

8 Lay the rods on top before the concrete dries. Position them so that they are an equal distance apart across the soffit

9 Taking care not to move the rods, fill the rest of the box with fresh concrete. Make sure that it is well compacted around the edges

Simon Butcher

10 Draw a wooden straightedge across the top of the formwork to level the concrete and remove any excess material

11 If the top of the lintel ends below the sides of the formwork, level off the concrete with a home-made rebated depth gauge

12 Leave the concrete to set for a day before knocking away the formwork. Allow seven to fourteen days before use

Important points

It is essential to take great care when positioning reinforced steel or wall ties. They should be placed where they are best able to absorb direct weight from above, but in such a way that the metal cannot rust.

When inserting reinforcement for a slab or lintel, position it low down, below the halfway line, where it will be most effective at counteracting stress. But never place it too near the bottom in case the weight from above pushes it through the concrete.

To prevent rusting, make sure that the reinforcement is completely surrounded with concrete. If it is exposed to the air it will quickly deteriorate and become ineffective. Burying steel rods is alway made easier if you cut them slightly shorter than the overall span of concrete.

If metal has to be left exposed—or there is any danger that it might become so—rust-treat it thoroughly before you position it. Use bitumen paint or a good quality rust retardant and coat the parts nearest the surface with two coats.

Finally, if you need to pour concrete on top of steel reinforcements, take care that these are not disturbed or moved in any way.

Installing a heated towel rail

● The advantages of installing a heated towel rail ● The types of rail available ● Identifying your hot water system ● Making the connection to the system ● Installing a towel rail in an existing central heating system

Once a luxury in its own right, the bathroom is now an area in which many householders indulge their taste for the luxurious. Yet, when they contemplate refitting the bathroom, surprisingly few people think of the one fixture that makes a really tangible contribution to bathing comfort: a heated towel rail.

As well as providing warm, dry towels at all times, a towel rail is among the most convenient ways of drying and airing washing. It is also an excellent means of fighting that familiar bathroom problem, condensation. A heated rail warms the atmosphere in the room and raises the temperature of wall and ceiling surfaces above dew-point (the temperature at which water condenses).

Types of heated towel rail

Heated towel rails come in all shapes and sizes, and vary widely in their complexity. If your bathroom already contains a radiator, all you need do is measure it and then buy one of the clip, clamp or hang-on rails that are available. Though not heated directly, these enable you to dry and warm towels in front of the radiator without impeding its main function.

Next on the list are electric towel rails—self contained units (generally oil-filled) which work on a similar principle to portable 'Dimplex' type radiators. These come into their own where it is either difficult or impossible to plumb in a hot water rail. Installing the supply for an electric towel rail is done in the same way as a bathroom wall heater (see pages 818 to 823).

A. Left: *A heated towel rail is both an attractive and practical addition to a bathroom. And, if you have a central heating system, you can instal the rail from branches off the hot water circuit so that it is controllable independently of the radiators*

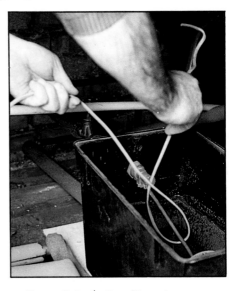

1 *Turn off the boiler, allow the system to cool down for several hours, then turn off the supply valve or tie up the cistern ball float*

2 *Attach a hose to the lowest drain cock in the system, run it to an outside drain, open all radiator valves then open the cock*

3 Cut copper tubing with a pipe cutter or a hacksaw fitted with a fine toothed blade and clean up the burr with a fine file

4 Bend copper tubing with a pipe bender, or use a spring or rubber 'bendable core' (to stop kinks) and manipulate the tube over your knee

5 Locate the primary circuit flow pipe (on the side of the hot water cylinder) and cut through it along a convenient straight run

Hot water towel rails are by far the most popular type. The plain tubular sort offer plenty of towel hanging space and generally produce enough heat to keep the average sized bathroom at a constantly comfortable temperature. They are plumbed in to the house hot water system—rather than the radiator circuit—so that they remain hot even when the heating is switched off. And, as most bathrooms have a hot water cylinder close at hand, this makes installation straightforward.

Some hot water rails include a radiator panel to provide extra heating facilities, but these can be fitted only to indirect type heating systems where there is no risk of them becoming clogged with scale. Tubular rails, on the other hand, can be installed in any

hot water system—direct or indirect—which incorporates a storage tank/boiler/hot water cylinder arrangement.

Identifying your water system

Before you plumb-in a hot water towel rail, it is obviously important to know what type of hot water system you have and to identify the pipes.

In the older, direct system, water heated by the boiler rises by thermal convection to the hot water cylinder. Here, it continues to rise until it passes out of the top (crown) to the hot taps, via the hot water supply pipe. Fresh water is fed to the system from the cold storage tank and enters via the base of the cylinder. From here, it sinks to the boiler under force of gravity.

If no water is drawn off the hot taps, the water in the system continues to circulate between the cylinder and the boiler. When hot water is used, fresh water is taken in and heated to the desired temperature.

Although simple, the main drawback of the direct system is scale. This is released every time fresh water is heated above about 60°C and clogs cylinder and boiler pipework alike. In the indirect system—most often found with central heating—the problem of scale is avoided by having two separate circuits. The first—known as the primary circuit—runs continuously between the boiler and cylinder. The water in it is always hot, but because it is never drawn off it needs to be heated only once. Consequently, it releases its scale the first time it is heated and from then onwards it is relatively scale-free.

The hot water cylinder in an indirect system contains a loop—the

heat exchanger—through which the hot primary circuit water passes. As it does so, it transfers its heat to fresh water fed to the base of the cylinder from the cold storage tank. This fresh water then becomes hot—but not hot enough to release scale—and rises out of the crown of the cylinder to feed the hot taps in the normal way. The cold feed, the outer part of the cylinder and the pipework supplying the hot taps comprise what is known as the secondary circuit.

Both direct and indirect systems contain vent pipes to guard against the build-up of excessive pressure. The direct system has a single vent pipe, rising from the crown of the cylinder, or the hot tap supply pipe, to above the cold storage tank. The indirect system has this pipe too, plus another rising from the primary circuit flow pipe to above the expansion tank.

The function of the expansion tank in an indirect system is to top up the water in the primary circuit, should some be lost by leakage or evaporation, and to allow for the slight expansion of the water as it is heated. The flow in the primary circuit may be by gravity—as in the direct system—or included in the radiator circuit and under pump pressure. In the latter case, a motorized valve distributes water from the boiler between the cylinder heat exchanger and the radiators as and where it is required.

Making the connection

Hot water towel rails work on the same principle as radiators, with two connection points for flow and return pipes. In both direct and indirect systems, pipes can run from these to

B. *A direct central heating system (1) has a single circuit in which the heated water is shared by the radiators and hot taps. Installing the towel rail circuit in the feed to the hot taps means that it works only when hot water is being taken (for example, at bathtime). Installing the towel rail in the hot water feed to the storage cylinder (2) gives it a constant supply of hot water and is more satisfactory. An indirect central heating system (3) has two circuits in which the water heated for the radiators is separate from the hot water circuit. The towel rail may be inserted in the hot water circuit (as in (1)), or (4) in the primary flow circuit which allows it to be controlled independently of both the radiators and the hot water taps for greater flexibility*

Making the connection

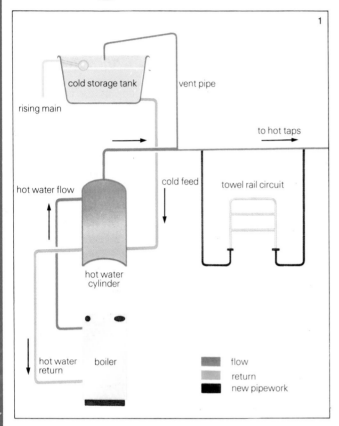

1

cold storage tank

vent pipe

rising main

to hot taps

hot water flow

cold feed

towel rail circuit

hot water cylinder

hot water return

boiler

flow
return
new pipework

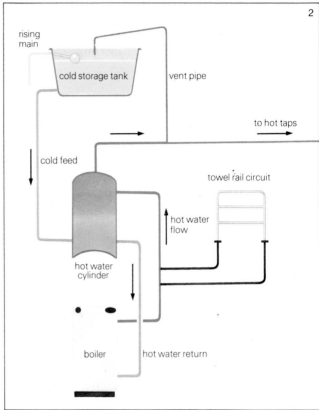

2

rising main

cold storage tank

vent pipe

to hot taps

cold feed

towel rail circuit

hot water flow

hot water cylinder

boiler

hot water return

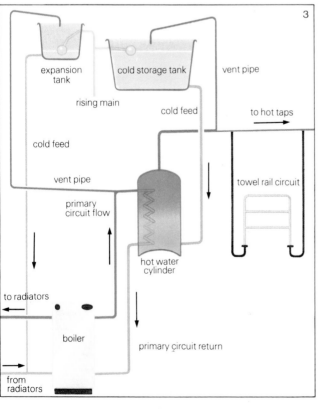

3

expansion tank

cold storage tank

vent pipe

rising main

cold feed

to hot taps

cold feed

towel rail circuit

vent pipe

primary circuit flow

hot water cylinder

to radiators

boiler

primary circuit return

from radiators

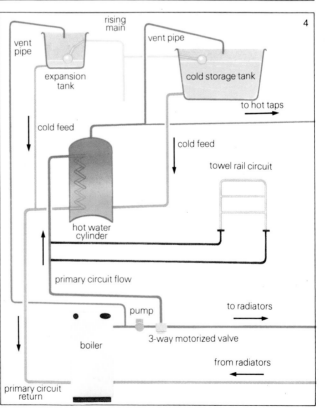

4

rising main

vent pipe

vent pipe

expansion tank

cold storage tank

to hot taps

cold feed

cold feed

towel rail circuit

hot water cylinder

primary circuit flow

pump

to radiators

boiler

3-way motorized valve

from radiators

primary circuit return

Venner Artists

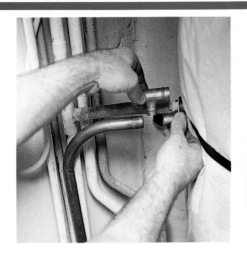

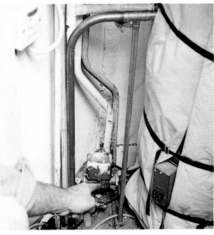

6 To take off the hot water you must insert T-connectors into the flow pipe. You can use either compression or capillary fittings

7 Fix the T-connectors in place, then run copper tubing from the site of the heated towel rail back to the cylinder and join it up

8 In the case of a solid floor, bury the piping in a channel 100mm deep. The pipe must be protected with a suitable insulating cover

intercept the hot water flow pipe between the boiler and the hot water cylinder. This pipe is cut, and T-shaped connectors inserted to make the final connections (fig. 6).

Obviously, it is absolutely essential to know which pipes are which before you connect to them. This may call for a bit of detective work—particularly in the case of an indirect system—before you go any further. But in any case you should aim to make the connections somewhere around the hot water cylinder. Here, the pipes are easier to identify.

Direct systems: Most direct cylinders have four pipes running from them (fig. B). Of the two near the crown, the lower is the flow pipe from the boiler which supplies the cylinder with hot water. The other is the hot water supply pipe, which supplies the hot taps and generally also holds the vent pipe. In some cases, the vent rises directly from the cylinder (in which case there will be a total of five pipe connections).

Of the two near the base, one is the cold feed from the cold storage tank and the other is the return taking back cooled water to the boiler.

Indirect system: Indirect cylinders have the same hot supply vent pipe at the crown and cold feed at the base as direct ones. But the primary flow and return pipes to and from the boiler generally run into the side of the cylinder and stand out from the rest of the pipework. An additional complication is the primary circuit vent pipe. This may pass near the water cylinder, or it may be connected to the flow pipe.

About the only safe way to identify

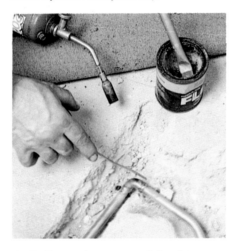

12 Route the copper piping into place then secure all the joints to complete the circuit. Try to use capillary fittings where you can

13 When all the connections have been made, you must clad the piping for protection where it passes through walls or floors

the pipes is to trace each one in turn and then lable it clearly somewhere near the connection point. Once you have the found the flow and return to the boiler, search for a suitable interception point on the flow pipe. This should preferably be on a straight, horizontal run. Make sure, too, that there will be room to work and that the pipe route to the rail will not be too tortuous.

Installation

Once you have decided on a site for the rail and identified the connection points, you are ready to begin installation. On all types of hot water system, the first job is to turn off the boiler and allow both pipes and cylinder to cool down. What you do next depends on the type of system.

Direct system: In this case it is preferable to turn off the cold water supply at the cold storage tank—rather than at the rising main—so that you will still have use of the kitchen cold tap. If there is no stop valve, tie up the ball valve in the closed position (fig. 1).

Drain the cold tank by opening all taps fed from it, then drain down the hot water system. Attach a hose to the drain cock, which should be located adjacent to the boiler in the return pipe, and having placed the other end of the hose at a suitable drainage point, open the cock.

With the cylinder empty, the hot water flow pipes can be cut using a fine toothed hacksaw and the T-shaped fittings connected. Since only one radiator/rail is to be served, the pipe

9 Mark the position of the towel rail fixing holes on the wall and floor, then drill them with a masonry bit and insert wall plugs

10 Secure the towel rail in place with the screws provided, but do not tighten the screws until each one has been started

11 Smear jointing compound on the threads of the towel rail connecting sockets before you screw on the wheel and lockshield valves

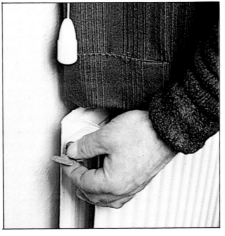

14 Turn on the water supply and allow the system to fill up. Check for any leaks, then make good with a cement/sharp sand mortar mix

15 Finally you must bleed each radiator in the system in order to expel any air which may have found its way into it

runs from the teeing points to the site of the unit can be safely made in 15mm copper tube.

Assuming that the bathroom is on the first floor, and the floor itself is a conventional joist and board structure, the pipes should run by the shortest possible route under the floorboards. If they must run across joists, notch them into the tops as described on page 1200. Where changes of direction are necessary, use elbow compression fittings or bend the pipe with a bending spring (see pages 50 to 54 and 194 to 197).

If running the pipes under the floor is not feasible, soldered capillary fittings are less obtrusive—and cheaper—than the compression type. Where changes of direction are necessary in surface piping, bend the pipe in

preference to using bulky ready-made fittings for a neater finish.

If the bathroom is on a solid ground floor, it may be possible to run the pipes in the ceiling void, then down to connect to the towel rail. The connections to the rail are made with normal radiator valve fittings, a wheel valve with a turntable head on the flow (hot supply) side, and a lockshield valve with a screw-fixed cap on the return side. These compression-joint to the pipes, which must be cut to length once the rail is in place.

Unlike radiators, which are usually hung on brackets fixed to the wall, towel rails—including those incorporating radiator panels—are fixed to the floor by screws passing through their flanged feet. Some also have flanges at the top so that you can fix

them to the wall for added stability.

With the unit fixed and the connections made, check that all taps and drain cocks are closed, open the air vent—normally located under the top rail of a towel rail—and restore the water supply. As the system fills, watch for water appearing at the rail vent. When it does so, close the vent, restart the boiler and run it for about half an hour. Then re-open the vent to release any trapped air in the towel rail itself, with a small pot under the valve to catch any water.

Indirect systems: Here, there is no need to shut off the water at the main cold storage tank or drain the hot water cylinder. Instead, cut off the supply to the expansion tank, attach a hose to the central heating system drain cock—which should be located on the boiler return pipe at its lowest point—and open the cock.

The water in the system should contain rust-inhibiting chemicals, and you may feel it worth collecting the drained water in containers to be put back into the system when you refill it rather than buy a new supply.

Having drained the system completely, proceed as for a direct hot water system. When the installation is complete, refill the system by restoring the cold supply at the expansion tank. After filling, turn all your radiator valves to the fully open position and bleed the radiators in turn to remove airlocks. When you are opening lockshield valves, count how many turns it takes, and afterwards close them by the same number. You may find that the system needs further bleeding after several days, but this is perfectly normal.

A coffee/games table

Although it is handy for coffee or occasional use, this versatile table has a hidden extra in the form of movable tops which turn it into a ready-made playing surface for cards, backgammon, chess or draughts

This attractive and versatile piece of furniture makes a very useful coffee table. And with its pine veneered surface and curving lines it looks unusual yet blends in well with modern furnishings.

Its versatility is extended by the removable tops, which you can simply lift out and refit to give you interchangeable boards for playing all kinds of different games. There is plenty of space below the top for storing all the playing pieces, cards and counters.

Most of the construction is in pine veneered chipboard. You can buy this in large sheets and cut out all the pieces, or use narrow standard width boards, large enough to cut each piece you need.

Unusually for a chipboard construction, some of the parts have a curved shape. These are not difficult to cut, but you will need to use care when finishing the cut edges with an iron-on veneer, to avoid splitting the veneer as you bend it.

Mark out the curved sections by using the squared up diagrams to scale up to full size. The rectangular parts can be cut quite simply.

Begin your assembly with the end rails and legs. Then fit these together with the two side rails and the stretcher rail. You can add the pegs to the rail after assembly, as they are mainly decorative. Check that the frame is square and leave to dry.

Add the two fixed tops and then the top supports, which hold the movable tops flush. The two pivoting supports are for use with the chessboard, since the thickness of the backgammon board underneath precludes fitting both tops together. Panel in the underside of the frame.

Make up the two movable tops. The first has pine veneer on one side and felt on the other. On the second, draw out your playing surfaces, score the lines and fill in with different coloured wood stains and a small paintbrush. You can of course adapt the design for any favourite games or even glue a paper games board in place on the top.

To finish the table, sand and seal the entire surface thoroughly. You can use lacquer or wax, but make sure you seal the tops or they will mark. It is a good idea to seal before fitting the felt.

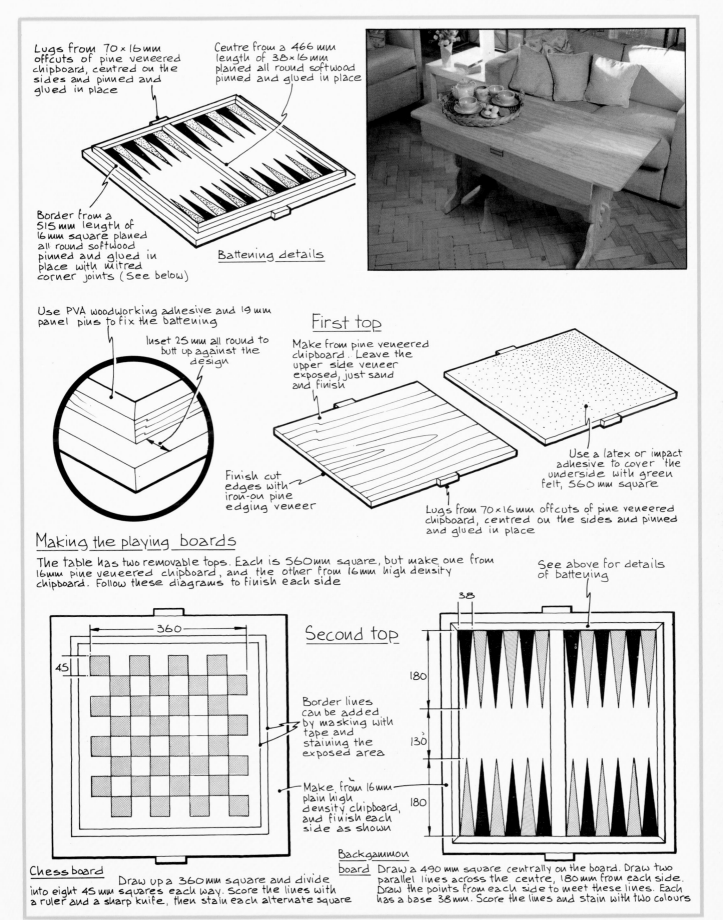

Lugs from 70 × 16mm offcuts of pine veneered chipboard, centred on the sides and pinned and glued in place

Centre from a 466mm length of 38×16mm planed all round softwood pinned and glued in place

Border from a 515mm length of 16mm square planed all round softwood pinned and glued in place with mitred corner joints (See below)

Battening details

Use PVA woodworking adhesive and 19mm panel pins to fix the battening

Inset 25mm all round to butt up against the design

First top

Make from pine veneered chipboard. Leave the upper side veneer exposed, just sand and finish

Finish cut edges with iron-on pine edging veneer

Use a latex or impact adhesive to cover the underside with green felt, 560mm square

Lugs from 70×16mm offcuts of pine veneered chipboard, centred on the sides and pinned and glued in place

Making the playing boards

The table has two removable tops. Each is 560mm square, but make one from 16mm pine veneered chipboard, and the other from 16mm high density chipboard. Follow these diagrams to finish each side

See above for details of battening

Second top

360

45

Border lines can be added by masking with tape and staining the exposed area

Make from 16mm plain high density chipboard, and finish each side as shown

38

180

130

180

Chessboard

Draw up a 360mm square and divide into eight 45mm squares each way. Score the lines with a ruler and a sharp knife, then stain each alternate square

Backgammon board

Draw a 490mm square centrally on the board. Draw two parallel lines across the centre, 180mm from each side. Draw the points from each side to meet these lines. Each has a base 38mm. Score the lines and stain with two colours

Project

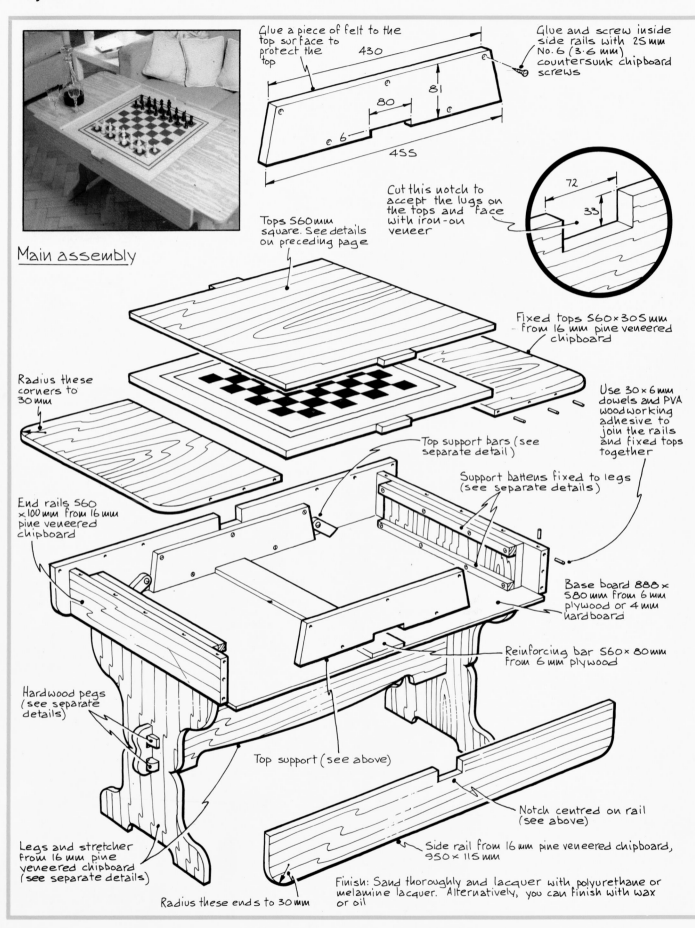

Glue a piece of felt to the top surface to protect the top

Glue and screw inside side rails with 25mm No. 6 (3.6mm) countersunk chipboard screws

430

81

80

6

455

Cut this notch to accept the lugs on the tops and face with iron-on veneer

72

33

Main assembly

Tops 560mm square. See details on preceding page

Fixed tops 560×305mm from 16mm pine veneered chipboard

Radius these corners to 30mm

Use 30×6mm dowels and PVA woodworking adhesive to join the rails and fixed tops together

Top support bars (see separate detail)

Support battens fixed to legs (see separate details)

End rails 560 ×100mm from 16mm pine veneered chipboard

Base board 888× 580mm from 6mm plywood or 4mm hardboard

Reinforcing bar 560×80mm from 6mm plywood

Hardwood pegs (see separate details)

Top support (see above)

Notch centred on rail (see above)

Side rail from 16mm pine veneered chipboard, 950×115mm

Legs and stretcher from 16mm pine veneered chipboard (see separate details)

Radius these ends to 30mm

Finish: Sand thoroughly and lacquer with polyurethane or melamine lacquer. Alternatively, you can finish with wax or oil

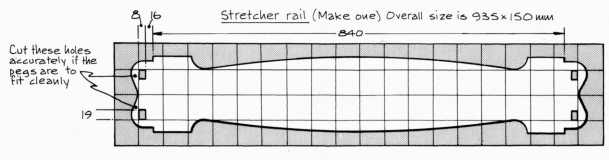

Stretcher rail (Make one) Overall size is 935 × 150 mm

8 16
840

Cut these holes accurately if the pegs are to fit cleanly

19

Cutting out the stretcher rail and legs

Use these diagrams to mark out sheets of 16 mm pine veneered chipboard for the curved sections of the table. Each square on the grid represents 50 mm on the finished part so square up your boards and copy the curve on each square. Use a jig saw, coping saw or bow saw to cut out the curves, keeping square to the work. Cover the cut edges with an iron-on pine veneer

Hardwood fixing pegs

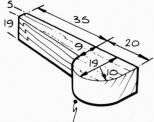

5
19
35
9
19
20
10

Make four pegs from 45 mm lengths of 19 mm square hardwood, such as beech. Push through the tusk of the tenons at each end after assembly and glue in place

Leg (Make two)

Overall size is 570 × 460 mm. Mark both legs together

Check the dimensions of this mortise slot against the tenons of the stretcher to allow for any inaccuracy in cutting

Leg fixing detail

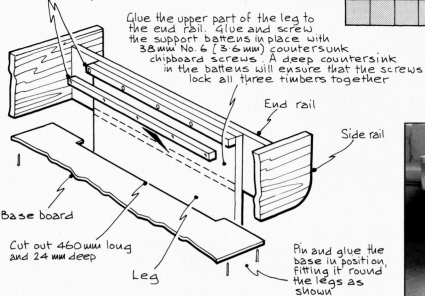

16mm square support battens, 460 mm long

Glue the upper part of the leg to the end rail. Glue and screw the support battens in place with 38 mm No. 6 (3·6 mm) countersunk chipboard screws. A deep countersink in the battens will ensure that the screws lock all three timbers together

End rail

Side rail

Base board

Cut out 460 mm long and 24 mm deep

Leg

Pin and glue the base in position, fitting it round the legs as shown

Project

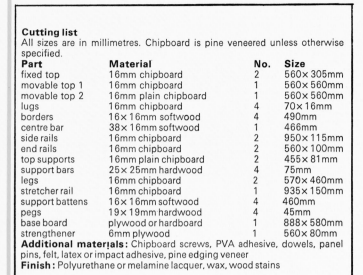

Cutting list

All sizes are in millimetres. Chipboard is pine veneered unless otherwise specified.

Part	Material	No.	Size
fixed top	16mm chipboard	2	560 × 305mm
movable top 1	16mm chipboard	1	560 × 560mm
movable top 2	16mm plain chipboard	1	560 × 560mm
lugs	16mm chipboard	4	70 × 16mm
borders	16 × 16mm softwood	4	490mm
centre bar	38 × 16mm softwood	1	466mm
side rails	16mm chipboard	2	950 × 115mm
end rails	16mm chipboard	2	560 × 100mm
top supports	16mm plain chipboard	2	455 × 81mm
support bars	25 × 25mm hardwood	4	75mm
legs	16mm chipboard	2	570 × 460mm
stretcher rail	16mm chipboard	1	935 × 150mm
support battens	16 × 16mm softwood	4	460mm
pegs	19 × 19mm hardwood	4	45mm
base board	plywood or hardboard	1	888 × 580mm
strengthener	6mm plywood	1	560 × 80mm

Additional materials: Chipboard screws, PVA adhesive, dowels, panel pins, felt, latex or impact adhesive, pine edging veneer
Finish: Polyurethane or melamine lacquer, wax, wood stains

When you are using the chessboard, the projection of the backgammon below means that only one top can be fitted, so use the support bars to create a flat surface by raising this top

Glue a piece of felt to the support bar to protect the top

Chess board

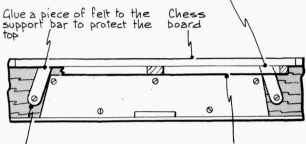

Fix the support bars so that when raised as shown, they support the top flush with the fixed tops

Battening of backgammon board

Cross sections

1st top   2nd top   Top support   Fixed top   End rail

Bevel top to 80°

Section I   Top support bar   Section II

Leg   Leg

570

25mm No.6 (3·6mm) domed head chipboard screw and washer

25 × 25mm hardwood, 75mm long

Support bar detail

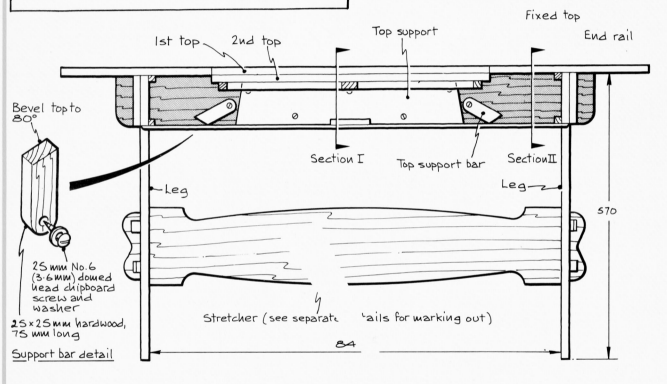

Stretcher (see separate details for marking out)

84

Top support

Support bar   1st top   2nd top   Side rail   Fixed top   Support battens

Section I

Section II

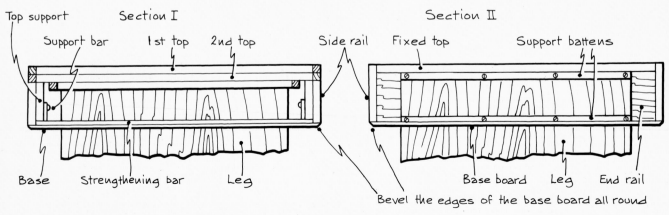

Base   Strengthening bar   Leg   Base board   Leg   End rail

Bevel the edges of the base board all round

Injecting a damp-proof course

Rising damp is an unpleasant and destructive problem which must be tackled as soon as it is discovered. However, by adapting a common garden pressure spray you can instal a chemical DPC quickly, cheaply and efficiently

Left: *Injecting the brickwork with a silicone-based fluid is, for the DIY enthusiast, the easiest and most certain way of dealing with rising damp. Using the ubiquitous garden pressure spray, the fluid can be injected quickly and economically*

Gavin Cochrane

The silicone injection system

Silicone is basically a wax with powerful water-repellent qualities and in DPC fluid, it is dissolved in a spirit base together with anti-fungal additives. To treat brickwork, holes are drilled into the walls, interior and exterior, all around the house at a certain level. Then the DPC fluid is pumped in until it displaces the water in the brickwork. Finally the spirit base evaporates, leaving a waxy gel inside the pores of the brickwork and mortar. This cuts off and reverses the wall's natural capillary action, forcing damp downwards and preventing the passage of external moisture.

Silicone DPCs are best installed in brickwork but they can be used also in some types of stone; they are effective for walls up to 450mm thick. A variant on the standard fluid contains a metallic additive which is specially formulated to provide a DPC through the rubble infill found between the two skins of brickwork in older, 'puddle' walls (though these are rare).

Identifying rising damp

If your house either has no DPC or appears to have a faulty DPC you must remedy the situation as soon as possible to prevent damp spreading.

To start with you should try and discover the age of your property. If it was built before 1875 there is almost certainly no DPC but of course, newer houses may also lack one. Look for a dark layer of slate between two courses of bricks near ground level.

The presence of rising damp is indicated by a number of possible symptoms: rotten wood at ground level; decorations stained by a water tide-mark, spreading upwards; soft, decaying plaster; mould or fungus growth on wall surfaces; wallpaper lifting from the wall or an unpleasant musty smell.

But it may be that the damp is caused by something relatively trivial, which can be remedied without recourse to a silicone installation. One possible cause is a pile of earth that has bridged the DPC (see pages 289 to

Rising damp is one of the most serious problems affecting older houses. It ruins decorations, creates an unpleasant atmosphere, causes musty smells, and threatens any adjoining woodwork. And the continued presence of damp in walls is likely to lead to either wet or dry rot in skirting boards, door and window frames, and structural joists.

Most houses built in the UK before 1875 were never given a damp-proof course (DPC). And many newer properties have DPCs which have failed through being breached by settlement cracks. Traditional DPCs consisted of a layer of either slate—which can crack—or bituminous felt—which can become brittle and crack after a time. Slightly less common was two or three courses of hard engineering bricks (which are impervious to water).

There are several ways of installing new DPCs in existing buildings:
● It is possible to cut out a layer of mortar and insert bituminous felt.
● Ceramic respirators can be inserted into the brickwork to carry damp away by evaporation.
● Copper wires can be plugged into the wall to drain off the tiny electric currents which encourage water to rise up the wall.
● The bottom courses of the brickwork can be injected with a silicone-based fluid.

For the DIY enthusiast, the last method is by far the easiest and most certain way of dealing with rising damp. The first method, although by far the most effective, is not practical for the average home owner.

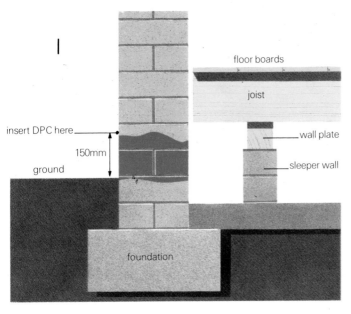

1

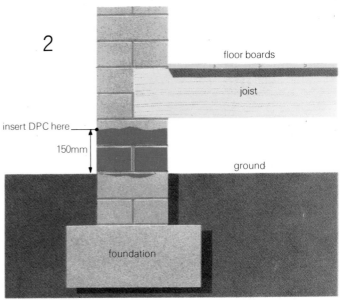

2

293). Another is a crack in the brick-work which runs through the DPC. In this case the remedy is simply to repair the crack and the DPC locally.

One common cause of damp is the DPC being bridged by external render-ing which has 'blown'—worked loose—allowing moisture to travel up the wall by capillary action.

Pre-installation treatments
The way that you tackle rising damp depends to a large extent on the construction of the lower floors, and on the type and thickness of the walls.
Solid floors: These may be wholly solid, concrete surfaced with tiles, or stone. They must incorporate a damp-proof membrane (usually a sheet of heavy gauge PVC or a layer of black bitumen-based compound) which meets up with the DPC.

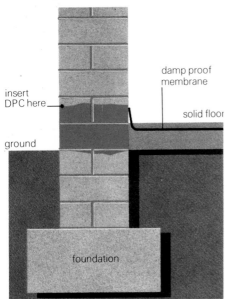

To test for rising damp in solid floors make a ring of putty on the floor and then press a sheet of glass firmly on to the ring in order to form an airtight seal (fig. B). If there is no adequate damp-proof membrane, con-densation will form beneath the glass within a few days.

Floors which lack a damp-proof membrane must first be levelled with a self-levelling compound (see pages 666 to 669) and then painted with two coats of damp-proofing fluid.

If there is a damp-proof membrane, make sure that it continues some way up the wall; if it does not, the margin between the floor and the wall must be treated before any replastering and after the DPC installation. Having cut away the damp wall plaster—to a height of at least 200mm above floor level—fill any gaps that are left in the

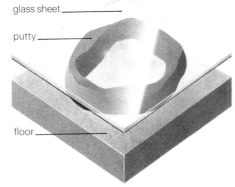

B. *Solid floors* (**left**) *must have a damp-proof membrane which meets up with the DPC in the walls. To test for rising damp, press a sheet of glass* (**above**) *on to a ring of putty. If con-densation forms beneath the glass, the floor lacks a proper DPC*

A. Above left: *The type of suspended floor that rests on a sleeper wall is much less threatened by rising damp than the type that is set into an ex-terior wall* (**above right**). *Test all timbers with a knife blade and replace any that are affected by wet rot—then instal the DPC*

brickwork with mortar containing a waterproofing additive. Then paint at least three coats of bituminous fluid along the outer edge of the floor, over the filled gaps, and at least 150mm up the wall. Take care to leave no gaps: damp can rise through the smallest gaps and thinnest layers.
Suspended floors: There are two main types of suspended floor. In type 1 (fig. A) the joists rest on a sleeper wall and in type 2 (fig. A) they are set into an exterior wall. Check which kind you have simply by lifting a couple of floorboards near to the edge of the floor and looking for the presence or absence of sleeper walls with a torch.

Type 1 floors are much less threat-ened by rising damp than type 2 because usually there is a thin bituminous layer between the brick-work of the sleeper wall and the timber itself. Push a knife into the timber on top of the wall which supports the floor joists (the wall plate): if it resists the blade you can be sure that it is free of rot.

In the case of type B floors you must test the joists themselves and use a torch to search for any signs of fungus and rot (see pages 492 to 495).

In the case of wet rot in type 1 floors you must completely replace all affected timber, then instal a DPC in both the sleeper and the outside walls.

If you have dry rot then you should call in a specialist firm to carry out the treatment (see pages 492 to 495). Make sure that the DPC is at least 150mm above the ground level in order to protect the walls, skirtings and decorations. If the timber shows no signs of rot, simply spray the timber with a preservative.

In the case of a sound type **2** floor with no DPC you must instal a DPC in the outside wall from below the joists to 150mm above ground level. This may involve lowering the ground level around the walls a little. But where rotten timber is encountered you must replace all the affected floorboards and joists, and spray the rest of the timber with a preservative. If you are in any doubt about the presence of dry rot, spray both the timber and the masonry with dry-rot fluid.

Walls below ground level: It is not possible to instal an effective DPC in any walls below ground level. However, in cases where there is a different ground level against one side of the house, there are two possible alternatives.

One method is to instal a continuous DPC following the ground, with 'verticals' linking the different levels (see fig. C). In this case any walls which cannot be protected by the DPC must be tanked internally against the damp. This is done with waterproof cement or bitumen waterproofer and is covered further on in the Repairs and renovations course.

The better method where the walls make direct contact with high banks of earth is to dig these away and form a trench around the house. Also, if possible, construct a small retaining wall to hold back the earth. You can then instal a continuously level DPC, which is less prone to being breached.

Installing the DPC

Professional installers pump the silicone fluid into the wall but although the pumps can be hired they are messy and tend to waste much of the fluid. Conventional DIY practice is to decant the fluid into the wall from inverted bottles and although this method involves little effort, penetration may not be thorough.

Probably the best method for all-round ease and efficiency is to inject the fluid from an ordinary garden-type compression spray. With this you simply remove the nozzle and insert the hose into a home brewing bung matched to the size of your pre-drilled holes.

The DPC fluid itself is generally available in 25, 5 and 2.5 litre drums.

You will need about one litre of fluid per 300mm length on an average, solid (225mm) wall.

Because you will need to drill a great many holes in the brickwork, it makes sense to hire a medium sized rotary hammer drill with pneumatic action and a clutch to save fatigue and jams. Buy a carbide-tipped masonry bit to match the thickness of the bung you are using, and make sure that it is long enough to penetrate the wall at an angle. Use bungs between 16mm and 20mm in diameter.

Preparing the walls

In order to ensure the success of the treatment you must remove any old or unsound plaster, the first 150–200mm of rendering, and repair any cracks in the wall. Pour a thin mixture of concrete grout into any cracks and allow it to set before injecting the DPC. Similarly, rake out and replace any crumbling mortar, and replace any badly damaged brickwork.

Note that old plaster on the other side of a party wall can bridge your DPC. In this case, you must tank the party wall up to at least 1m from the ground and if the damp is particularly bad, extend your DPC over three courses of brickwork.

C. Left: *Where the ground level varies you must instal a continuous DPC, following the ground. The best way to protect walls below ground level (**below**) is to dig the earth away from the wall and then build a small retaining wall*

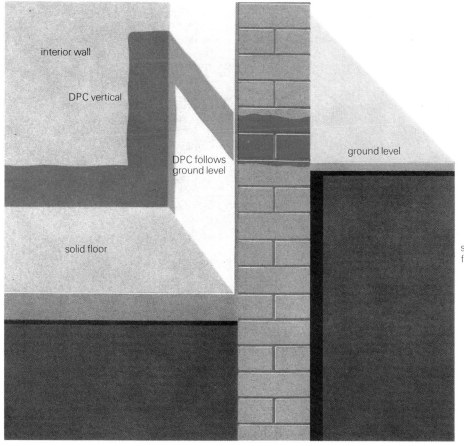

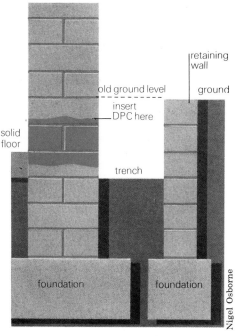

1 The equipment you need to instal a chemical DPC with a garden spray. The rubber gloves and eye protectors are essential equipment

2 Remove the nozzle from the spray and connect a suitable piece of plastic tubing to the spray rod. Use a copper tube to connect the bung

3 Remove wallpaper from the wall. Damp paper should be easy to move, but if not, wet it and then scrape it off with a wide knife

When treating party walls, the DPC fluid may affect your neighbour's decorations, and you would be wise to obtain his permission before starting.

Having prepared the walls for treatment, drill the holes. Standard solid walls, up to 225mm thick, need only a single hole, but wider and cavity walls must be drilled from both sides. The holes must be inclined downwards about 15°, and should stop about 25mm short of the other side. Internal walls may be only one thickness of brick, and in this case drill shorter holes accordingly.

Drill the holes about 100–125mm apart, staggered in two courses of mortar as shown in fig. D. If you need to instal any lengths of vertical DPC, drill staggered holes as shown in fig. D. Drilling from the inside of the wall ensures that the correct courses

of brickwork are treated, but if you have to drill the outside wall take care to check the internal and external ground levels to make sure that you are working on the correct courses of brick. Measure down rather than up.

When you are installing a DPC in a semi-detached or terraced house you must drill extra verticals along the margin with the neighbouring houses which do not have a DPC, to stop the neighbouring walls from bridging your own DPC. You must drill these holes on the outside, at least 1m from the ground in a staggered pattern as shown in fig. D.

Injecting the DPC

Start by hammering the bung tightly into the hole; but avoid applying so much force that the hole is squashed. Insert the hose of your spray almost as

far as the end of the hole, then simply pressurize the spray container and pump DPC fluid into the wall until the surrounding brickwork is saturated. This takes between two and five

D. A large number of holes must be bored in the brickwork, so it is a good idea to hire a heavy-duty hammer drill. It is normal to drill holes from the inside of the wall in order to ensure that you are treating the correct courses. Because of the lower pressures of the spray injection method, you must bore the holes at least 16mm wide to avoid air locks. If you can only obtain much larger bungs, you may open the first 20mm of the holes to the appropriate size. The incline of the holes is not critical, but it is as well to slope them to ensure a thorough application to the brick courses

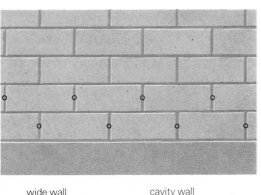

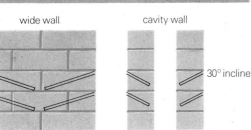

wide wall   cavity wall

30° incline

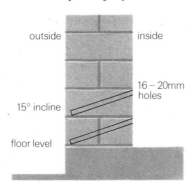

outside   inside

16 – 20mm holes

15° incline

floor level

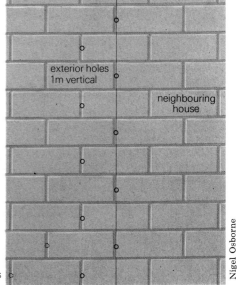

exterior holes 1m vertical

neighbouring house

interior holes

Nigel Osborne

4 *Use a bolster and club hammer to hack away all the plaster to a height of at least 1m above the skirting board timber*

5 *Bore a series of pilot holes in the wall with a small bit. Then use a 16mm bit to open out the holes, using tape to gauge the depth*

6 *In the case of a terraced or semi-detached house, you must bore a series of holes vertically to prevent any bridging of your DPC*

minutes and is apparent when the fluid comes to the surface of the wall.

When every hole has been treated, you must allow the walls to dry out for at least three weeks; in humid places like cellars, complete drying may take several months.

Making good

As the walls dry out, white efflorescent salts form on the surface of the brickwork. Clean the walls with a wire brush and then wait a few days to see if any more salts emerge. If you plaster over the salts, they will cause the plaster to lift from the wall.

When the wall is clean, paint it with a coat of DPC fluid up to a height of 1m on the outside brickwork and all the exposed brickwork on the inside.

On the outside walls you must now fill any holes with mortar and replace any rendering that you removed with a mixture containing waterproofing agent. On inside walls it is a good idea to first coat the brickwork with either a skim coat of waterproof cement render or a bitumen paint. Finally replaster using two coats of lightweight gypsum plaster with a waterproofing additive.

7 *Fill the garden spray bottle with the silicone liquid, then pressurize it. If the chemical spills on you, wash it off imediately*

8 *Insert the bung into the hole, then put the copper tube into the bung. Turn on the spray and watch for signs of liquid on the brickwork*

Caution

DPC fluid is a dangerous, inflammable substance. It must not be inhaled, and must be kept away from skin at all times. Always wear eye protection and heavy duty rubber gloves when handling it. Take care to remove all floor coverings and protect any rubberized or ashphalt surfaces: DPC fluid dissolves ashphalt and will bond linoleum to the floor.

9 *Having inserted the DPC, you must allow the wall to dry out for at least three months. Wet the holes to provide a key for the mortar*

10 *Finally make good the holes with mortar, replace any rendering with a mixture containing a water-proofing agent, then replaster*

Gavin Cochrane

Decorating with cork

● Cork tiles ● Cork sheeting ● Colours and finishes ● Preparing surfaces for cork ● Working with cork ● Tiling walls and floors ● Hanging sheeting ● Protective finishes for cork ● Finishing the surface

Cork is one of the most versatile of all home decorating products. It gives a hardwearing finish to floors, walls and ceilings, yet looks equally good covering furniture or small household ornaments. And few materials can reproduce the look and feel of a natural material combined with a range of subtle textures and colours in the same way that cork can.

Because it contains a large number of tiny air pockets, cork also makes a large contribution to insulating your home against cold and helps to cut down noise. A floor covered in 5mm thick cork is 70 per cent more effective in reducing heat loss than a comparable vinyl or quarry tile finish; it is also a lot quieter underfoot. Walls and ceilings are likewise better protected from noise and cold if they are covered in cork—especially the thicker variety of tile.

Left: *Cork tiles for use on floors can be bought coated with a layer of PVC or polyurethane. This gives protection to the floor surface*

Types of cork

Cork sheet is manufactured by bonding together granules of the bark of the cork oak tree under heat and pressure. The resulting material is then cut into a number of different forms so that it can be handled and applied more easily.

Tiles: Cork is usually bought in tiles 300mm square which vary in thickness from 4mm to 20mm. Although some builders' merchants do sell tiles separately, they are usually supplied in packs containing between nine and 20 tiles. The advantage of this form of cork is that it can be applied to all surfaces—some tiles are made especially for floors, others for walls and ceilings—yet can be easily fixed and fitted around awkward corners.

Planks: Many manufacturers now

Right: *Tiles for walls are available in a wide range of shades and textures and make an attractive decorative finish*

Clive Helm

1487

produce a range of rectangular cork tiles—called planks—measuring either 910mm × 300mm or 900mm × 150mm. These can be fixed to give a 'decking' effect or laid in patterns similar to those used when laying brick paths (see pages 784 to 788).

Sheeting: Cork is often applied to walls and ceilings in the same way as wallpaper and rolls of sheet cork are available to do this. Although great care needs to be taken when fixing this delicate material in place, it is well worth the effort since fewer joints are visible and greater insulation is achieved because of this.

Finishes and colours

Cork tiles, slabs and sheeting are usually bought untreated so that they can be waxed or varnished once they are fixed in place. But all types of cork are available ready-coated in a hardwearing protective layer of PVC, polyurethane or wax. Many of the more expensive sealed tiles and slabs have a second protective layer under the cork—usually made of PVC—which acts as a moisture barrier and helps give added grip and stability to the fitted material.

When buying cork you can also choose from a wide variety of shades, textures and patterns. Plain colours range from the classic honey shade most commonly associated with cork to a deep chocolate brown—with practically every shade in between.

Geometric and random patterns are produced by combining accurately cut slivers of different coloured cork and this technique is also used to give a textured finish to the cork. More recent is the production of randomly-spaced cork superimposed on a number of different coloured backgrounds (see page 1487).

Preparing bases

Cork is an absorbent, pliable material and unless it is applied to a perfectly flat, dry and sound base it will quickly deteriorate. You will greatly extend the life of your surface covering by spending time beforehand in strengthening and preparing the base to which it is to be fixed. The approach you use will vary according to where the cork is to be fitted.

Timber floors: This is the best surface of all on which to apply cork—providing you make sure that the surface is perfectly flat. Hammer any protruding nails into the floor, punching them well below the level of the boards if necessary. Use filler to make good any hollow areas and smooth these level with an abrasive block once the filler has thoroughly hardened.

The timber floor you want to cover can often be in very poor condition with broken and splintered timbers and an uneven surface. If this is the case, you must lay sheets of hardboard or plywood over the damaged floor to form a sound base.

Cut the sheets so that they cover the whole floor and butt neatly against each other and around the edge of the room. Fix them securely into place with 20mm galvanized nails randomly spaced at 300mm intervals.

Concrete floors: These must be level, clean and absolutely free of damp before cork is fixed to them. Check the floor carefully, looking for patches of damp or areas where the surface is uneven or crumbling.

Floors which do not have an adequate DPC should have one added before work continues, but as an added protection against damp, coat

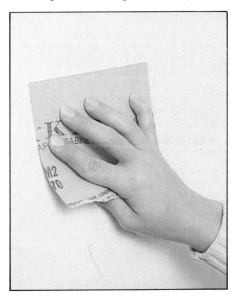

1 *Before applying cork tiles to a painted wall, abrade the surface with glasspaper to provide a key for the cork adhesive*

5 *When applying cork slabs, mark around the first piece beforehand to make it easier to position the piece correctly*

6 *Spread adhesive over the first part of the area to be covered, working outwards from the centre to ensure an even application*

7 *Hold the first piece of cork in place on the wall then press it home, making any minor adjustments in position before the glue sets*

the area with bitumen paint before fixing the cork. To ensure adequate protection, apply two coats—leaving the first to dry thoroughly before painting the second. Once the area is thoroughly covered, leave the floor for at least 24 hours and check for recurring damp before continuing.

On uneven concrete surfaces use a self-levelling compound to smooth out dips and bumps (see pages 666 to 669). Once the compound has settled, leave it for two to three days to harden completely before fixing the cork to the floor.

Flaking or porous concrete floors should be stabilized and primed before work begins using a proprietary concrete stabilizing solution and a primer suitable for concrete floors.

Vinyl tiles: If the floor is already covered with vinyl tiles, these can be left in place providing they are firmly fixed and there is an effective DPC. Check the floor carefully, refixing loose tiles with impact adhesive. Then, to help the cork to adhere, rough up the existing tiles by rubbing them all over with steel wool.

Quarry tiles: Cork can be applied directly on top of quarry tiles but a careful check should be carried out for traces of damp before this is done. Even if the quarry tiles do not feel damp to the touch they may not have an adequate DPC; and if there is any doubt about this once checks have been carried out, seal the floor with two coats of bitumen paint.

2 Rub down the surface thoroughly with a clean, damp cloth to remove any remaining traces of dirt or particles of existing decoration

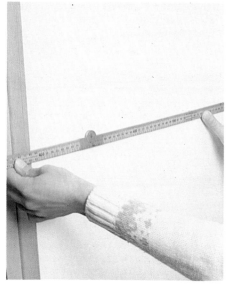

3 To make sure of an equal trim at each end of the tiles or slabs, measure the width of the area and calculate the amounts to be cut

4 Drop a plumbline from the top of the surface, then make a pencil mark along it to provide a vertical guide for positioning the cork

8 When you come to apply the final row of slabs at the top of the area, carefully measure the space to allow for an exact cut

9 Mark the cut on to the cork slab with a pencil or marker, then use a handyman's knife against a steel straightedge to cut the material

10 Press the cut piece of cork slab into position, making sure that its lower edge butts evenly against the edge of the tile below

Walls and ceilings: A newly plastered wall or ceiling takes at least two months to dry out and should be left to set before cork is applied. This will allow any expansion or contraction of the material to take place during which time hairline cracks may appear in the plaster. Repair these with a filler and smooth the surface level with abrasive paper mounted on a block once the filler has hardened.

On older walls and ceilings, strip the surface clear of wallpaper or other coverings and rub it all over with abrasive paper to remove flaking paint and flatten surface bumps.

If the wall or ceiling is damp—indicated by the presence of powdery white stains—check that the wall and roof DPCs are sound. If not, a new DPC should be inserted or the wall drylined before the cork is fixed in place (see pages 789 to 793). As an added safeguard apply two coats of bitumen paint to the surface in the same way as the floor (see above).

If the wall or ceiling appears loose or flaking once the surface covering is removed, stabilize it with a coating of PVA bonding solution. When this has dried, check the plasterwork carefully for any further signs of loose material or flaking paint and apply a second stabilizing coat if necessary.

Essential equipment
Not many tools are needed when working with cork but a few are essential to obtain good results.
Cutting tools: To mark and cut cork accurately and neatly, you need a rule, a pencil or felt-tipped marker, a sharp handyman's knife and a steel straightedge.
Adhesive: Most hardware stores and builders' merchants which supply cork will also stock a specially-made impact adhesive to fix it in place. This does not contain water—which might affect any expansion or contraction of the cork once it is positioned. And because it is only spread on to the surface to be covered and not on the cork backing, it is quicker to use and allows the cork to be repositioned once it has been applied.

Cork adhesive is usually supplied in one litre plastic tubs—enough to secure about three square metres of cork. A serrated spreader—used to apply the adhesive—is generally included with each tub but this can easily be made from a 300mm square piece of hardboard or thick plastic. To do this use scissors or a sharp knife to cut 10mm deep notches spread evenly across one side of the material.

Decorating rooms with cork
Once you have chosen the type of cork you want and prepared the base thoroughly, calculate the amount of material you will require. When using sheet cork this is a relatively easy job but tiles or slabs may need more careful planning.

Draw the area you want to cover on a sheet of paper and then, starting from the centre, subdivide this into a number of squares making each square equal to one tile or slab. In this way you can calculate exactly the amount of material you need to buy and also plan any unusual patterns which you might want to create.

Once the number of tiles or slabs has been established you can make a final decision on which colour or texture cork you want and order accordingly from your local store or builders' merchant. To lay the cork, work outwards from the centre of the area you want to cover, applying the adhesive firmly as you go (see pages 380 to 385).

When the covering is completed, and tiles neatly trimmed to fit around the edges, leave the area for about one and a half hours. Then press the cork firmly into place, by walking over it if it is on the floor or pushing against it with both hands if it has been applied to a wall or ceiling.

If you are using sheet cork to decorate a wall or ceiling, this should be applied in a similar way to wallpaper (see pages 82 to 87 and 876 to 881). However, unless you are working with paper-backed cork (fig. 15), spread the adhesive over the surface to be covered. Smooth each length into place with a clean cloth or a mohair roller and butt joint it as you progress.

Leave the material for about one and a half hours before fixing it finally into place. Use a hard rubber roller or a hand-held cloth to push each length hard against the wall or ceiling until you are sure it is firmly held. Stick any edges or corners that are loose into place with a contact adhesive at this point.

Sealing and finishing
If you have invested in cork which already has a protective coating, all that is needed is to wipe the surface clean with a damp cloth and leave the adhesive to dry. However, untreated cork—unless it is on an area where it will not be damaged—should be levelled and sealed so that it is adequately protected from wear and tear. This is especially important in places such as floors where the material is likely

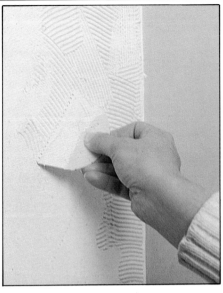

11 *When you have covered the first section, apply further adhesive over the remaining area using the notched spreader*

15 *Fold the strip of cork sheeting over itself, concertina-fashion, to make it easier to handle, then carry it to the work area*

to be subjected to a great deal of stress in use.

Leave the cork for at least 24 hours before finishing so that any sealant which seeps down between joins in the cork will not react with the adhesive and break the bond. Then, with a piece of fine sandpaper, work along each of the joints sanding down any overlapping or protruding material until the whole surface is smooth and level.

During laying—or maybe even

12 When applying the bottom row of slabs, again make sure that the edges butt evenly to achieve a neat and professional finish

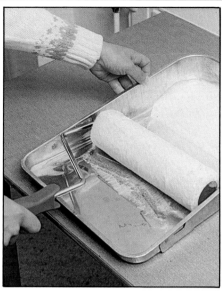

13 When hanging paper-backed cork, the adhesive should be applied to the back of the sheeting itself rather than to the wall surface

14 Pour a small amount of the ready-mixed PVA adhesive into a paint tray—then use a paint roller to coat the back of the material

16 Having correctly positioned and aligned the strip of sheeting, firmly roll it down and smooth it into place with a felt roller

17 To make sure that the edges of adjacent strips join evenly, and to prevent them from tearing, roll them down with a wooden roller

18 Where the sheeting meets the angle of a window recess, or a similar obstacle, trim off the edge with a pair of sharp scissors

before this, during manufacture—the surface of the cork is bound to have picked up marks and scuffs. Remove a certain amount of these as best you can by rubbing gently with a fine grade of sandpaper.

When you are satisfied that the whole area is clean and smooth, remove any cork dust with a vacuum cleaner and a moist rag. Take great care from now on not to dirty the cork or accidentally get dust on it until it is finally sealed.

The cork can be sealed with a light coating of wax if it is in an area where it is unlikely to be easily damaged; but for surfaces such as floors, a number of coats of polyurethane lacquer is essential. Try to select a lacquer which will give good long-term protection such as a two-pack polyurethane or a hardglaze.

Follow the manufacturers instructions when using a lacquer, leaving plenty of time for drying after each coat and then rubbing the surface with

very fine wire wool before applying the next. As many as five coats may be required with some types but this will be well worth the effort for a hard-wearing, long-lasting finish.

If the cork has been sealed with care, it should last for a very long time and require only a wipe with a damp cloth to remove stains and dirt. But if the area should need resealing, use fine wire wool to rub the cork clean and to key the surface for further lacquering.

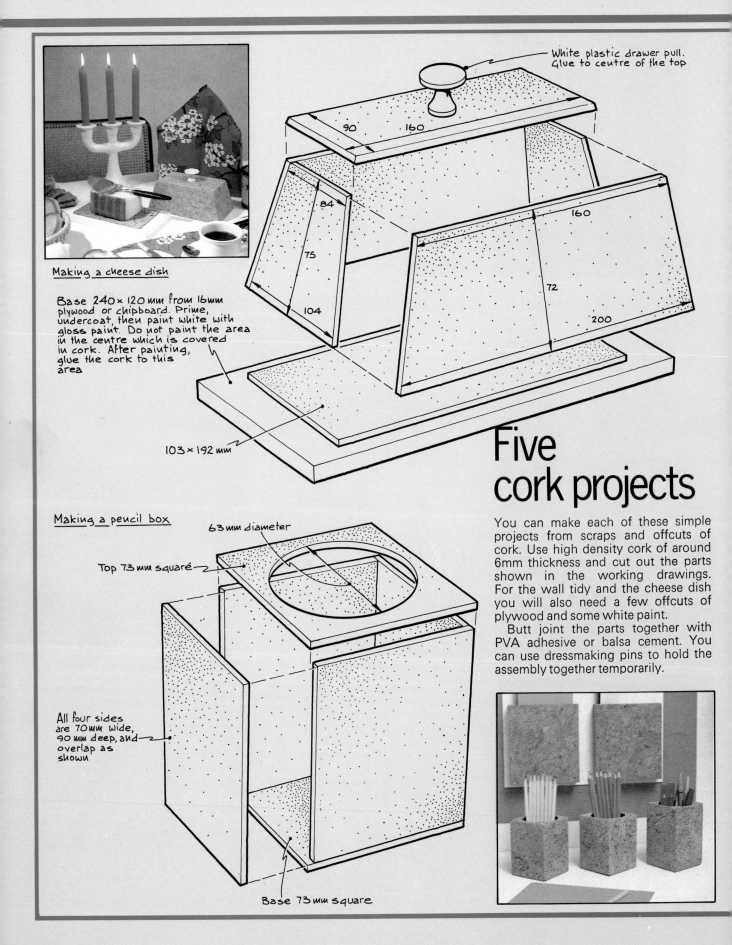

Making a cheese dish

Base 240 × 120 mm from 16mm plywood or chipboard. Prime, undercoat, then paint white with gloss paint. Do not paint the area in the centre which is covered in cork. After painting, glue the cork to this area

103 × 192 mm

White plastic drawer pull. Glue to centre of the top

90   160

84

75

104

160

72

200

Five cork projects

You can make each of these simple projects from scraps and offcuts of cork. Use high density cork of around 6mm thickness and cut out the parts shown in the working drawings. For the wall tidy and the cheese dish you will also need a few offcuts of plywood and some white paint.

Butt joint the parts together with PVA adhesive or balsa cement. You can use dressmaking pins to hold the assembly together temporarily.

Making a pencil box

63 mm diameter

Top 73 mm square

All four sides are 70 mm wide, 90 mm deep, and overlap as shown

Base 73 mm square

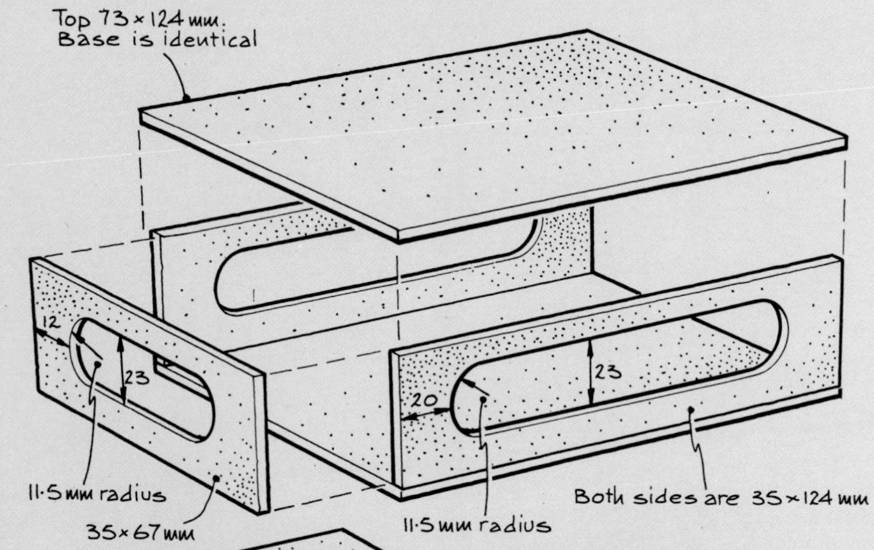

Top 73 × 124 mm.
Base is identical

12

23

11·5 mm radius

35 × 67 mm

11·5 mm radius

20

23

Both sides are 35 × 124 mm

47 mm
diameter

Making match box holder
and cigarette box

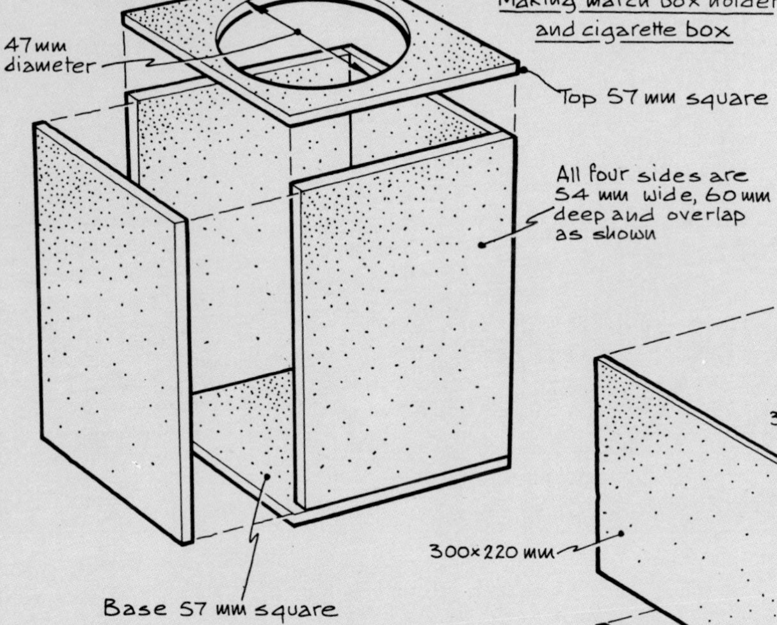

Top 57 mm square

All four sides are
54 mm wide, 60 mm
deep and overlap
as shown

Base 57 mm square

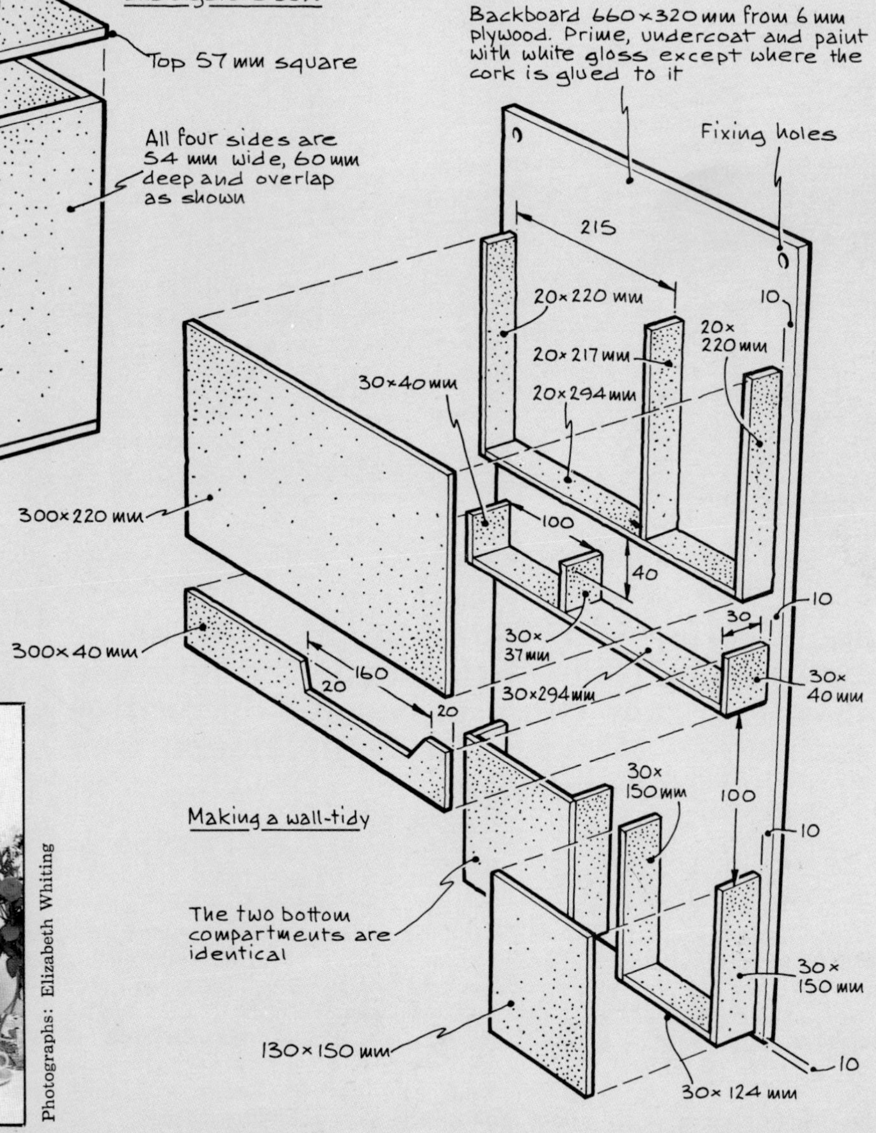

Backboard 660 × 320 mm from 6 mm
plywood. Prime, undercoat and paint
with white gloss except where the
cork is glued to it

Fixing holes

215

20 × 220 mm

20 × 217 mm

20×
220 mm

20 × 294 mm

30 × 40 mm

300 × 220 mm

100

40

10

300 × 40 mm

20

160

20

30×
37 mm

30 × 294 mm

30

10

30×
40 mm

100

30×
150 mm

Making a wall-tidy

The two bottom
compartments are
identical

10

30×
150 mm

130 × 150 mm

30 × 124 mm

10

Photographs: Elizabeth Whiting

Advertising Arts

Interior doors

The doors inside your home might seem to be merely functional, but with a little thought and consideration, they can also become decorative and attractive features to complement and enhance your overall decor

Though the prime purpose of internal doors is functional—keeping draughts out, smells in and generally making rooms more cosy—they can also be made interesting and attractive features in themselves.

Many modern homes suffer from cheap, dull, flush doors which would greatly benefit from an unusual decorative effect. And in some cases it might even be worth replacing a door to give the room new perspective.

If you are replacing an internal door, because an existing one has been damaged, an internal redevelopment calls for one, or simply to improve a rooms appeal, it is worth considering the many and various types available before making your final choice. But whether you want a simple panelled door or one of the more decorative styles like louvred, glazed or folding, be sure it will look right with the rest of the decor before deciding finally.

Choosing a door

Panelled doors consist of thick surrounds into which four, or more, thinner panels are set—often surrounded with narrow architraving or beading. They are particularly attractive because of the detail and look good whether left natural, stained or varnished, or simply painted. The architraving can be picked out in a contrasting colour for a more effective and stylish finish.

Louvred doors, with their rows of tiny shutters, add interest to a room and also permit a certain amount of ventilation. Most are sold in natural wood, which may be stained or painted, though this can be a fiddly process. If you want a louvre effect without the draughts, you can also buy louvre panels which may be fitted on to an ordinary flush door.

Dutch or stable doors are divided horizontally across, so that the top half can be opened while the bottom remains closed. They are usually made from solid wood, if bought ready-made, although some are available with a glazed panel in the upper half.

These doors are particularly useful between a kitchen and eating area where you can create a hatch effect for serving food by opening just the top half. This is also good for a playroom where it is possible to keep an eye on the children while working in an adjoining room.

Glazed doors come in many styles and have the advantage of allowing light to filter through from either side. But while glass doors look very attractive they are also potentially hazardous and should be sited with care, particularly where there are children in the house.

Small areas of glass are less vulnerable than large ones, but in any case it is best to fit special safety glass or wired glass which is tough and remains in position when shattered. Frosted or etched glass is less likely to be crashed into than plain and gives a degree of privacy while still admitting plenty of light.

Mirrored doors give an impression

Far left: *The painted border around the door frame accentuates and draws attention to the unusual shape of this kitchen door.* **Above left**: *White paint makes a perfect surround for a door decorated to match the walls. Small glazed panels above the door allow for extra light.* **Left**: *Louvred saloon style doors are perfect for this small bathroom. Curtains may be pulled across for extra warmth and to close off the adjoining bedroom*

Bill McLaughlin

Elizabeth Whiting

made of wood or metal-framed glass and come in many styles. The folding type may have one or more folds, depending on the width they will span; the number of sliding doors needed will also depend on the width of the door opening.

These doors are particularly useful where a room is used for two purposes as they can double as room dividers. Most types require a track along the ceiling and floor for the doors to run in.

Concertina doors fulfill a similar function as folding and sliding doors in terms of space making but, as their name implies, fold together like a concertina. They can be made either of plastic, which is fairly cheap and

Bill McLaughlin

Above: *A glazed panelled door is useful between a kitchen and dining room, particularly where one of the rooms lacks natural daylight*

of space and look particularly impressive by artificial light. Sited where they reflect from a window, they can also improve the brightness of an otherwise dark area. However, mirrored glass tends to be a little disconcerting in places where people are likely to see themselves reflected very frequently. If you are not too sure about the effect a mirrored door will create, try hanging a lightweight mirror at waist to shoulder height on the door to see if the reflections disturb you.

Bear in mind, too, that mirrored glass tends to show every finger mark so it might be wiser to choose a patterned or variegated design rather than plain silvered. Tinted shades of bronze and gold tend to cast a warmer glow and reflect images less vividly.

Folding and sliding doors can be real spacemakers, especially in small rooms where you can use the space normally left free for opening the door to fit in extra furnishing items.

Folding and sliding doors may be

comes in a limited range of colours, or, for a more attractive—and more costly—finish, of wood. Because of their wipe-clean surface, plastic concertina doors are particularly useful for bathrooms and kitchens.

Decorating doors

Doors are rarely given the consideration they deserve when it comes to redesigning and decorating a room—most simply being painted to match other paintwork. However, there are many other more interesting ways of decorating a door—or indeed, of disguising one.

Paint is the obvious and possibly easiest choice for decoration. And

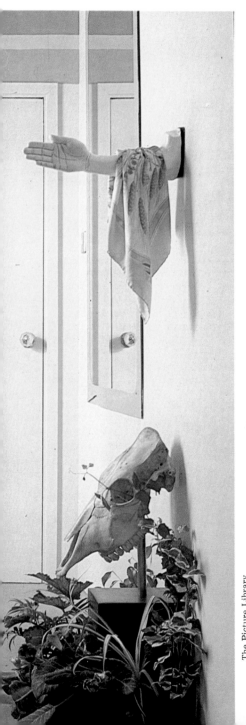

The Picture Library

with the wide range of colours available it is not difficult to find one that will match your decor exactly. But because doors get a lot of handling, it is best to choose a gloss finish which can be easily wiped clean of dirty finger marks.

A plain painted door will look much more decorative given a contrasting wallpaper or hand-painted border. Or you might try something more creative and paint on a simple flower design or motif to match the wallpaper. If you want something more dramatic a single stripe or geometric pattern going across or around the door can look most effective.

Wallcoverings can also be used on

Left: *A plain flush door can become an interesting and dramatic feature simply by adding a striped border, in toning colours, around the door frame and continuing it around the walls at skirting level.* **Below:** *Panels of fabric wallcovering give this glazed door a particularly bright and attractive finish, adding style to the hallway*

Elizabeth Whiting

doors—either to highlight or disguise them. For instance, panelled doors can look most effective with the panels decorated in paper to match the walls, and the surround painted in a toning or contrasting colour.

On the other hand, if you want to disguise the fact that there is a door in the room at all, you can cover it with the same material as on the walls to make it blend in with the walls and virtually disappear.

You will need to use a stronger adhesive than ordinary paste for applying wallcoverings to a door and if the paper is not of the spongeable or vinyl type it will need a coat of clear lacquer to help protect it. Remember, however, that lacquer will slightly alter the colouring of the paper, so avoid this method if you want the door to blend in with the walls.

Another decorative idea is to use fabric on the door—perhaps to match your curtains and cushions. Use a latex adhesive to apply it, but avoid fabrics which are very thin, or light in colour as the adhesive may show through. Alternatively, use small gimp or panel pins and stretch the fabric across the door top and bottom. Large headed pins may also be used to form part of the decorative effect. Once the fabric is fixed in position, spray on a protective coating of stain and water repellent to prevent it becoming too marked or stained.

Cork is another good material for decorating a door and it can also be used as a pinboard. Thin cork sheeting may be cut to the exact size of the door, though if you want it to double as a pinboard, use thicker cork tiles.

A more unusual decorative finish can be achieved by stencilling a design onto the door. You can either buy ready-made stencils or make your own—stencil paper is available from most good art shops together with suitable brushes. Once you have completed the design, give it a protective coating of lacquer.

Another fun idea, but one which will take time and patience, is a large decoupage on the door. Build up a collection of pictures, postcards, birthday cards and any photographs you particularly like and paste them together on the door to form a decorative surface. When the door is completely covered, coat the pictures with polyurethane varnish. Apply a second coat when the first has dried thoroughly then rub it down until smooth. Repeat the process, one coat at a time, until you get an even surface without any of the paper edges coming through.

More drylining systems

Simon Butcher

● **Drylining methods for walls that may not be perfectly true** ● **The insulation benefit** ● **Finding the high spots in a wall** ● **Drylining with fibreboard pads** ● **Using metal furring** ● **Fixing wallboard temporarily and permanently**

Above: *The metal furring system of drylining is ideal for walls that are uneven over their entire surface. The furrings themselves are bonded to the wall in dabs of a special adhesive. Ordinary wallboard can then be fixed to them using self-tapping screws*

Drylining provides a practical alternative to plastering for a professional wall finish. Mounting plasterboard on a suitable timber support frame was explained on pages 1022 to 1027. This method is a perfectly satisfactory way of mounting plasterboard, providing the walls on which it is to go are true and flat. For uneven walls, two alternative methods of mounting plasterboard can be used.

One of these employs a system of metal channels (furrings) bonded to the wall—in effect to duplicate many of the functions of an ordinary timber frame. The other method entails using small bitumen-impregnated fibreboard pads at selected points on the wall.

Plasterboard is then attached to these support systems—by screws in the case of metal furring, and by dabs of adhesive or plaster on the wall in the case of pads.

Each system is capable of taking up surface irregularities of up to 25mm in overall depth. This may not sound much, but it does get round the problem of 'building up' the support timber when a straightforward timber frame is used for drylining a wall (see pages 1022 to 1027, and 1042 to 1047 for conventional drylining). And both systems can be used for drylining walls with perfectly level surfaces—additional cost is the only problem.

Tapered-edge wallboard 900mm wide and thermal board 1200mm wide can be used with the fibreboard pads. The metal furring system is designed for use with 12.7mm tapered-edge wallboard, vapour-check board, and thermal board of various thicknesses, and can handle boards 1200mm wide.

Both systems are ideal for drylining 'cold' walls to the exterior, because the air gap provides an additional

insulating barrier and can be used for concealing services such as pipework and wiring. However, make sure that heavy fixtures are fitted direct to the wall, to avoid strain on the wallboard or the support system used, and that all work of this nature is completed before drylining begins.

Finding the 'high spots'

As in the case of drylining with timber framework, the first step is to determine the position and number of 'high spots' in the wall you are drylining. Use a long timber straightedge and spirit level to locate each high spot (see Plastering 2). Then mark the floor below and ceiling above them clearly in chalk. The marks are used to determine the position of the new wall base allowing for the combined depth of the support system, wallboard and adhesives.

If you are using metal furring, this allowance is about 12mm for standard wallboard, and 15mm for thermal board. Taking this into account, make new marks 12mm or 15mm in front of the highest point marks on the ceiling and floor and extend across the breadth of the wall, marking lines on both the ceiling and the floor. These are used to set the furring level.

If fibreboard pads are being used, the high spot itself is used as a guide for the level to be set. The method of fixing the wallboards in position—dabs of plaster or adhesive—takes up much of the irregularity likely to be encountered in a typical wall, but even so the individual pads have to be plumbed to a constant depth. The high spot pad is provided with only a smearing (3mm) of plaster or adhesive to fix it in place. All other pads in the same line vertically are then stuck into position, and their distance from the wall adjusted to match that of the high spot pad by using thicker dabs of the fixative. Because the alignment procedure is an integral part of the fixing procedure, you need only to find the high spot at this stage.

Drylining with fibreboard pads

Pads are arranged to cover a wall vertically at 450mm centres, starting either at an opening such as a window or door, or from a corner (fig. A). The vertical separation between pads should not exceed 1m, and additional pads are required for window reveals wider than 450mm. For reveals narrower than this, plasterboard can normally be fixed simply by generous dabs of adhesive or plaster.

Start the fixing sequence by marking the walls, ceiling and floor at the various 450mm centres. Afterwards, locate and mark the high spot.

You can use dabs of *bonding coat* ('Carlite'), *finish plaster* ('Thistle-board') or a suitable *multi-purpose adhesive* ('Gyproc') for fixing the pads in position. Setting time varies from one hour for the first to two hours for the others. Bear this in mind should you be able to complete the pad fixing quickly—the pads must be allowed time to bond to the wall before the boards are fixed in place.

Fix the first pad in position on the high spot using a minimum amount of plaster or adhesive. Its distance from the wall is used straight away to determine the setting of the three or more pads on the same fixing line.

Apply a dab of plaster or adhesive to a point about 250mm from the ceiling, and along the fixing line. Apply another, 100mm from the floor, and a third at an intermediate position (or two more if the separation is greater than 1m). Push a fibreboard pad into each dab, at this stage hard enough only to hold them in place.

Next, using the timber straightedge in conjunction with a spirit level and a plumbline, plumb vertically and sideways from the high spot pad to the ceiling pad in the fixing line. Push this into the fixative until it is exactly level with the high spot pad. If necessary, remove the pad and add more plaster or adhesive to build up additional support.

Then plumb downwards and sideways to set the floor pad in the fixing

1 *Find the high spots on the wall using a spirit level and straightedge, then mark lines on the ceiling and floor above and below them*

2 *Swing the straightedge across the wall as shown and make sure its leading edge does not extend past the floor and ceiling lines*

3 *For metal furring, next mark the fixing lines for the vertical channelling at 600mm centres using a soft pencil or chalk*

4 *Mark them on the ceiling too so that you know where the furrings are when you come to fix the boards in position later*

5 *To fit the channelling, start by applying thick dabs of the special adhesive at 500mm centres along the first fixing line*

Simon Butcher

6 *Then press a length of the furring against the dabs and check it for vertical alignment with your spirit level*

7 *Finish by pressing the straightedge against the channelling until its leading edge lines up with the ceiling high spot line*

8 *Fix subsequent runs of channelling in the same way, checking across them with the straightedge to ensure they are in the same plane*

line. When this is level with the high spot pad, carefully push home the intermediate pad using the straightedge until it is level with the rest. You must take care not to disturb any of the pads in the process, as they are now used to align all the remaining fixings on that particular wall.

With the pads in position, carefully hold the straightedge against them

and mark off its leading edge at both the ceiling and the floor. From these two marks draw guidelines across the ceiling and floor to coincide with each of the vertical fixing lines (fig. 7).

Choose a fairly distant fixing line (a separation of three lines, 1800mm, would be ideal) so that alignment errors are minimized, and then proceed to fix the pads of this line in

A. Below left: *In the fibreboard pad system of drylining, the boards are held by dabs of adhesive. The pads themselves take up any unevenness and provide backing support* **B. Below right**: *The metal furring system uses vertical channels and horizontal stops bonded to the wall with a special adhesive. Boards are then screwed into the metal furrings*

FIBREBOARD PADS

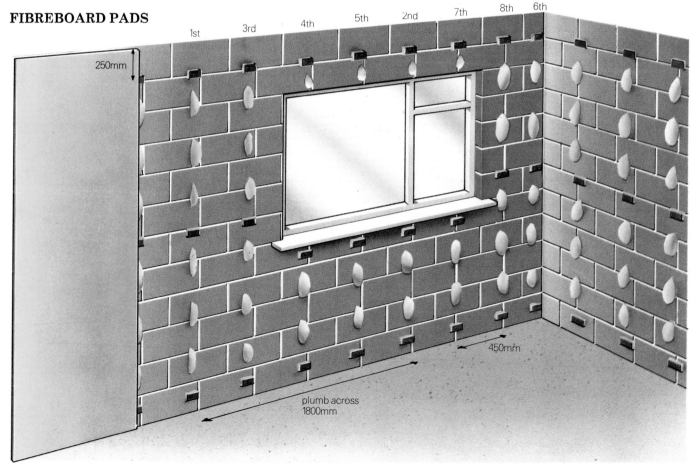

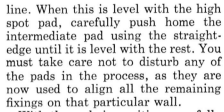

Simon Butcher

9 *Then apply dabs of adhesive in between them—25–30mm above and below floor and ceiling level—to hold the horizontal runs of furring*

10 *These runs, or stops, add rigidity to the finished wall. Press them on to the adhesive in the same way as the vertical channelling*

11 *Using the straightedge, force them down against the wall until they are level with the channelling. Mark their positions on the ceiling*

position, applying dabs of fixative and pads at top, middle and bottom as before. Hold the straightedge against the fixing line so that its leading edge coincides with the guidelines you have just marked, and at the same time use it to push the three pads level with each other.

If you have taken care in the marking of the guidelines, these three

pads should be level with the three original pads.

These two sets of ceiling, middle and base pads can then be used to level the pads of the fixing lines in between (fig. A). Apply plaster and pads to all the fixing points. Run the straightedge horizontally between the ceiling pads of the first and second fixing lines and, without disturbing

these, carefully push the intermediate pads until they are level. Do exactly the same for the horizontal lines of middle and base pads. This completes the pad fixing for a 'panel' of wallboard 1800mm wide.

The pads of the second fixing line (fig. A) can be used to originate a new panel by producing a further fixing line 1800mm (or as far as possible)

METAL FURRINGS

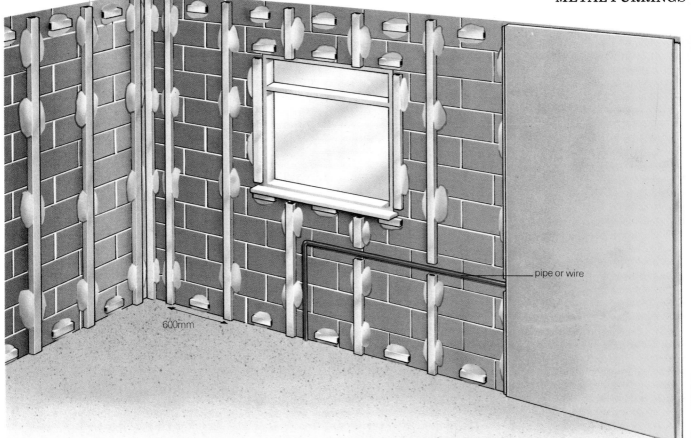

600mm

pipe or wire

Bernard Fallon

12 *A footlift like this is a useful device for manoeuvring the board into position. Check it is aligned correctly before fixing*

13 *Using the marks on the ceiling to locate the runs of channelling, screw the first board in place with special drywall screws*

14 *If you have a great deal of wall to cover, a power-operated screwdriver attachment is ideal for speeding up drylining work*

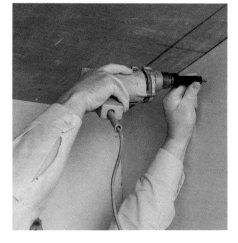

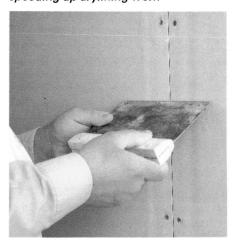

15 *Fixings are made at 300mm centres along the channelling, but no nearer to the edges than 10mm or the board may be damaged*

16 *When you come to fix subsequent boards, make sure they butt tightly against the previous ones and are aligned top and bottom*

17 *Once all the boards are in place you can use standard plaster-board jointing methods to hide the gaps and the screw fixing holes*

away from them. Any remaining fixing lines are then levelled in exactly the same way as the other intermediate fixing lines. Accuracy of the levelling procedure on the new panel can be checked as you go by observing the relationship of the straightedge to the pads which have already been levelled in the first panel.

Fixing the plasterboard
When the pads are firmly bonded to the wall, you can proceed to fix the wallboard in position using the same plaster or adhesive. Apply large, vertical dabs between the pads and cover an area sufficient for one board fixing at a time, always starting at a corner or opening. The depth of the plaster or adhesive dabs must exceed that of the pads, but their width need

not exceed 50–70mm. To avoid bridging joints, try to keep the dabs clear of the eventual board edge.

When the dabs for one board have been applied, carefully offer up the wallboard. This should be cut about 12mm short of the actual wall height, and apertures for fixtures and fittings made beforehand (see pages 1022 to 1027 for details).

On the presumption that a skirting-board will be fitted, arrange for the cut edge to be floormost. Edge the first board into position against the dabs of fixative with the aid of a footlift (fig. 12), and then use the straightedge to tap the board firmly against the pads themselves. Providing you spread the load along the straight-edge—and hence across the board—considerable pressure can be applied without risk of damage.

The plaster or adhesive dabs are thus forced flat against the rear of the board, and this adhesion is normally strong enough to keep the board in position. As you apply the final pressure, use the footlift to raise the board tightly against the ceiling and to see that the edges remain plumb and central to the line of vertical pads.

Permanent or temporary secondary fixings are then made to prevent the board slipping during the two hour drying period. Special double-headed nails can be obtained for temporary fixings; permanent fixing nails are carefully indented so that the nail heads may be spotted later. Be careful not to break the paper surface of the board when nailing.

Second and subsequent boards are treated individually, each being carefully butted to the edge of the previous one. Fit the facing boards below and above a window last. External and internal angles are treated as described above.

Should you decide to use thermal board instead of standard wallboard, follow the same procedure but employ 600mm fixing centres (boards are 1200mm wide) and secondary fixings—the latter to reduce fire risk.

Using metal furring
The metal furring system uses two types of component: *channelling* for the vertical fixing centres (every 60mm for 1200mm board); and *stops*, which are used horizontally to support the board ends top and bottom (fig. B). Multi-purpose adhesive ('Gyproc') with a drying time of two hours is used to bond the channelling and stops securely to the wall.

First of all establish the high spot and mark continuous lines on the ceiling and the floor corresponding to the leading edge of your straightedge.

The vertical channelling is set at 600mm centres in plain walling, but because board edges need support, internal and external corners must be carefully considered when marking up the position of the centres. Channelling should be brought as close as possible to the edge of the board in either instance. There is a slight complication with external corners in that the facing board must always be wide enough to take in the depth of the reveal board, its furring, and the adhesive. For this reason, you should work from the corners to determine the setting out of the board fixing centres, and mark these on the floor and ceiling as well as on the wall.

Apply dabs of adhesive along the vertical lines. These need not be continuous—you can allow gaps of as much as 500mm between dabs of about 250mm length—but they must be deep enough to fill out the perforated rear of the channelling or the bond with the wall will not be strong enough. Bear in mind also that the distance between the deepest part of the wall and the back of the channelling must not exceed 25mm.

When a line of adhesive is complete, cut the furring to length (it is available in lengths of 2260mm) and push it into position on the dabs of plaster, taking care not to take its leading edge past the lines you have marked on the ceiling and floor. Use a spirit level to ensure that it remains perfectly vertical at all times.

If channelling has to cross wiring or pipework, simply cut the length into as many pieces as is necessary to complete the vertical run (fig. B). But take particular care to ensure that you know where the junctions fall and that you do not accidently screw or drill through the services when you come to fix the boards.

When all the channels have been fixed into position, apply dabs of adhesive to fix the stops. These should be located 25mm–30mm from the ceiling and floor. Use a straightedge to tap them level with the vertical furring. Then use a straightedge, line and spirit level to check the overall alignment, breaking down and repeating any part of the system that is out of line. Leave the channelling to bond to the wall before attempting to fit the wallboard over the top with the screws provided in the metal furring kit.

Fixing the wallboards
Wallboard is fixed to the metal furring by special *drywall screws* (available in various lengths), which are both self-drilling and tapping. The 2mm size is suitable for 12.7mm board.

Start by accurately aligning the edge of the first board with the centre of the furring. The board does in fact cover three furrings if your system has worked out correctly, so each board has three vertical fixing lines. Fix the boards at 300mm centres, but take care not to come any closer than 10mm to the edges or you may damage them irreparably.

Cut the board to length and use a footlift and offcuts of wood to wedge it tight against the channelling and firmly against the ceiling.

End the fixing of each board by screwing it to the stop at the top and the bottom. All screws should be driven very slightly below the paper surface of the board to enable you to 'spot' them later.

The next board is lightly butted in place and its edge carefully aligned to the centre of the metal furring. If necessary, correct small vertical alignment errors by leaving a gap between the boards. Use wedges and offcuts to hold the board in the desired position while the fixings are made. Subsequent boards are then added in order.

Window reveals and soffits normally require only narrow sections of board, and it is usual to mount these directly on pads of adhesive rather than on small sections of furring.

Once the boards have been mounted, normal methods of jointing and spotting can be used to complete the drylining (see pages 1042 to 1047).

18 *The pad method. First find the high spots and mark up the wall. Then spread adhesive on the pads and apply them—starting at the high spot*

19 *Press the pads on the wall at the marked points (see fig. B) then use a straightedge to level them with the high spot pad*

20 *To hold the boards temporarily while the adhesive between the pads sets, nail through into the pads with double headed nails*

Simon Butcher

Tool box and tool carriers

Organize your tools with these practical carriers and tool box. They are all quite simple to make, and for the carriers you can use offcuts and scraps of wood

Keeping your tools tidy helps to keep them in good condition—and if they are all ready to hand it helps you to work more efficiently too.

There is ample room in this tool box for a comprehensive kit of wood-working tools, each in its own place. The two tool carriers are ideal for jobs which you have to do outside the workshop—at locations where you need just a few selected tools and materials.

All three are quite simple to make, although the tool box has a more complicated dovetailed frame. All of them use the minimum of materials, and you can probably make the carriers from offcuts and scrap.

Both the tool carriers are made in a similar way. The main difference is in the dimensions and the divisions fitted in the smaller one. The larger tool box also has strengthening blocks fitted to the corners. The joints are simple glued butts, reinforced with carefully inserted pins.

Cut out all the parts from plywood. There is no reason why you cannot alter the dimensions slightly to suit pieces of wood which are available, or to suit the size of particular tools. Glue and pin the box together and fit the dowel handle in place.

There is no real need to finish the wood at all, but it is a good way to use up scraps of paint or lacquer left over from other jobs. It is a good idea to leave the centre of the handle unpainted as it gives a better grip.

The tool box is a basically simple construction, but it is complicated by the dovetailed corners. Although these give a much stronger frame, if you prefer you can replace them with box joints or even butts, reinforced with corner blocks.

Make the rectangular frame first, taking care to keep the corners square. If you are using dovetails, note that one of the upper joints is wider than the rest. This is to allow for the saw cut which separates the lid. Make this when the frame is dry.

Fit the plywood front and back panels, which are glued and pinned in place. Glue and pin the hinge fillets along the edges of the lid and fit the piano hinge.

Make up the two drawers and fit their runners. You can add divisions as you require. Fit the bracket for the hand brace. If you wish, you can make a similar bracket for a coping saw. Fit turnbuttons inside the lid, positioning them to suit your saws.

Finish all the timber with lacquer, then add clips and a handle.

Cutting list (tool box)
All sizes are in millimetres. Timber is planed all round (PAR).

Part	Material	No.	Size
top & bottom	175×19mm softwood	2	800mm
sides	175×19mm softwood	2	500mm
back	4mm plywood	1	800×500mm
front panel	4mm plywood	1	800×100mm
lid	4mm plywood	1	800×400mm
hinge fillets	50×16mm softwood	2	768mm
drawer sides	75×16mm softwood	4	758mm
drawer ends	75×16mm softwood	4	125mm
drawer bases	4mm plywood	2	764mm
runners	25×25mm softwood	4	140mm

Additional materials: Timber offcuts for brackets, piano hinge, screws, pins, PVA adhesive, suitcase clips, handle
Finish: Polyurethane or melamine lacquer

Cutting list (large tool carrier)

Part	Material	No.	Size
base	6mm plywood	1	488×288mm
sides	6mm plywood	2	500×100mm
ends	6mm plywood	2	288×235mm
corners	12×12mm softwood	4	94mm
handle	19 or 25mm dowel	1	520mm

Additional materials: PVA woodworking adhesive, panel pins

Cutting list (small tool carrier)

Part	Material	No.	Size
base	6 or 4mm plywood	1	370×198mm
sides	6 or 4mm plywood	2	370×40mm
ends	6 or 4mm plywood	2	198×105mm
handle	19 or 25mm dowel	1	390mm
dividers	6 or 4mm plywood	2	96×38mm

Additional materials: PVA woodworking adhesive, panel pins

Ray Duns

Workplan

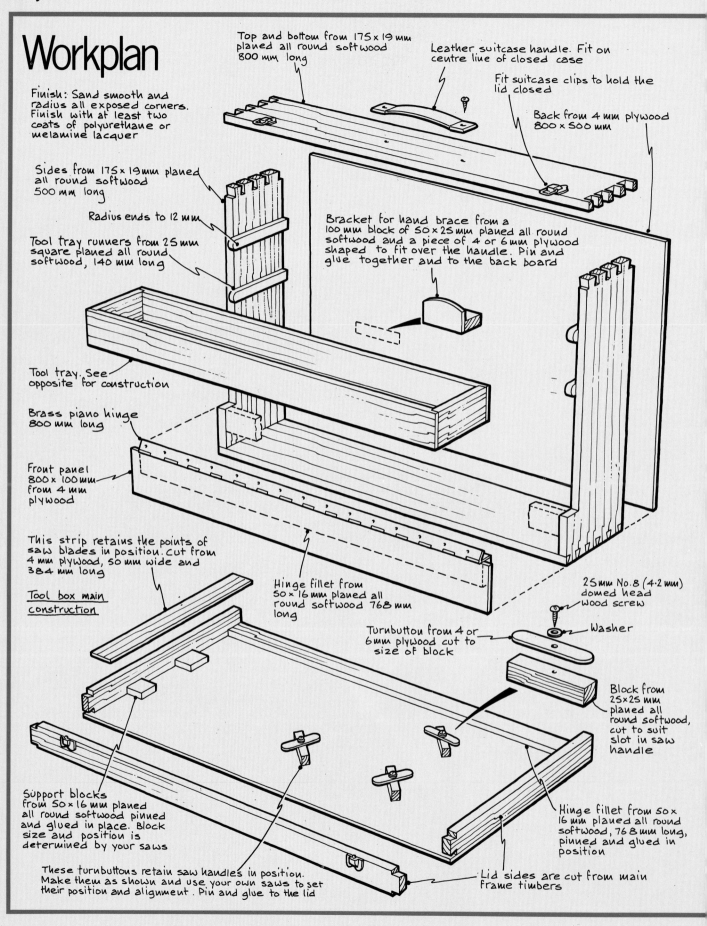

Finish: Sand smooth and radius all exposed corners. Finish with at least two coats of polyurethane or melamine lacquer

Sides from 175 x 19mm planed all round softwood 500 mm long

Radius ends to 12 mm

Tool tray runners from 25 mm square planed all round softwood, 140 mm long

Tool tray. See opposite for construction

Brass piano hinge 800 mm long

Front panel 800 x 100mm from 4 mm plywood

This strip retains the points of saw blades in position. Cut from 4 mm plywood, 50 mm wide and 384 mm long

<u>Tool box main construction</u>

Support blocks from 50 x 16 mm planed all round softwood pinned and glued in place. Block size and position is determined by your saws

These turnbuttons retain saw handles in position. Make them as shown and use your own saws to set their position and alignment. Pin and glue to the lid

Top and bottom from 175 x 19 mm planed all round softwood 800 mm long

Leather suitcase handle. Fit on centre line of closed case

Fit suitcase clips to hold the lid closed

Back from 4 mm plywood 800 x 500 mm

Bracket for hand brace from a 100 mm block of 50 x 25 mm planed all round softwood and a piece of 4 or 6 mm plywood shaped to fit over the handle. Pin and glue together and to the back board

Hinge fillet from 50 x 16 mm planed all round softwood 768 mm long

Turnbutton from 4 or 6 mm plywood cut to size of block

25 mm No.8 (4·2 mm) domed head wood screw

Washer

Block from 25 x 25 mm planed all round softwood, cut to suit slot in saw handle

Hinge fillet from 50 x 16 mm planed all round softwood, 768 mm long, pinned and glued in position

Lid sides are cut from main frame timbers

Advertising Arts

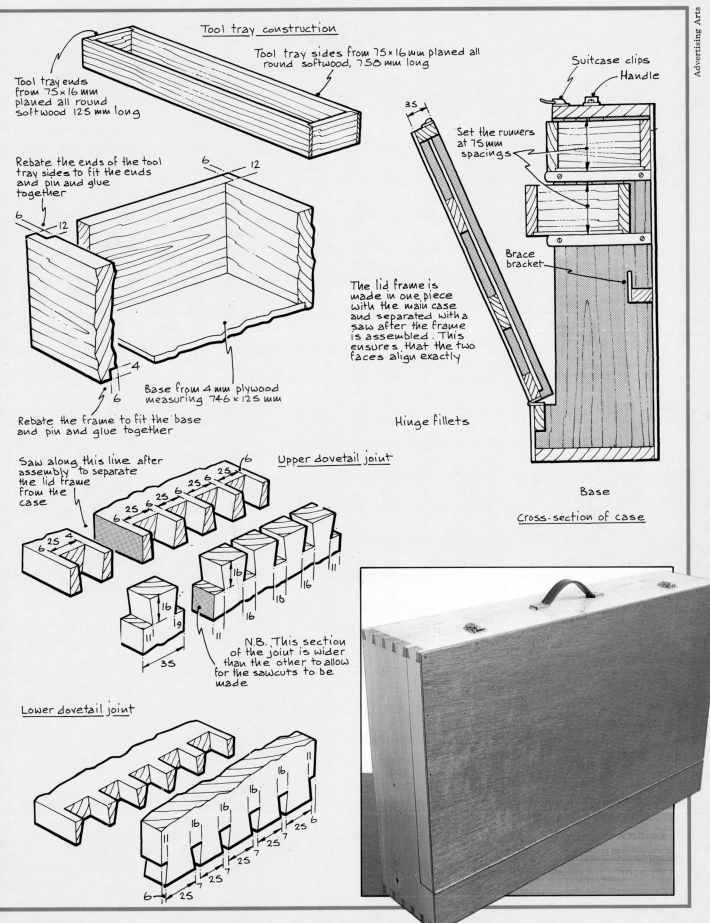

Tool tray construction

Tool tray sides from 75×16mm planed all round softwood, 750 mm long

Tool tray ends from 75×16 mm planed all round softwood 125 mm long

Rebate the ends of the tool tray sides to fit the ends and pin and glue together

6   12

6   12

4

6

Base from 4 mm plywood measuring 746 × 125 mm

Rebate the frame to fit the base and pin and glue together

Saw along this line after assembly to separate the lid frame from the case

Upper dovetail joint

25 6 25
25 6 25
25 6
6   25 4
6   25

16
9
11
35

16
16
16
16
11
11
11

N.B. This section of the joint is wider than the other to allow for the sawcuts to be made

Lower dovetail joint

11
16
16
16
11
11
16
16
25 6
25 7
25 7
25 7
6   25

35

The lid frame is made in one piece with the main case and separated with a saw after the frame is assembled. This ensures that the two faces align exactly

Hinge fillets

Suitcase clips
Handle

Set the runners at 75 mm spacings

Brace bracket

Base

Cross-section of case

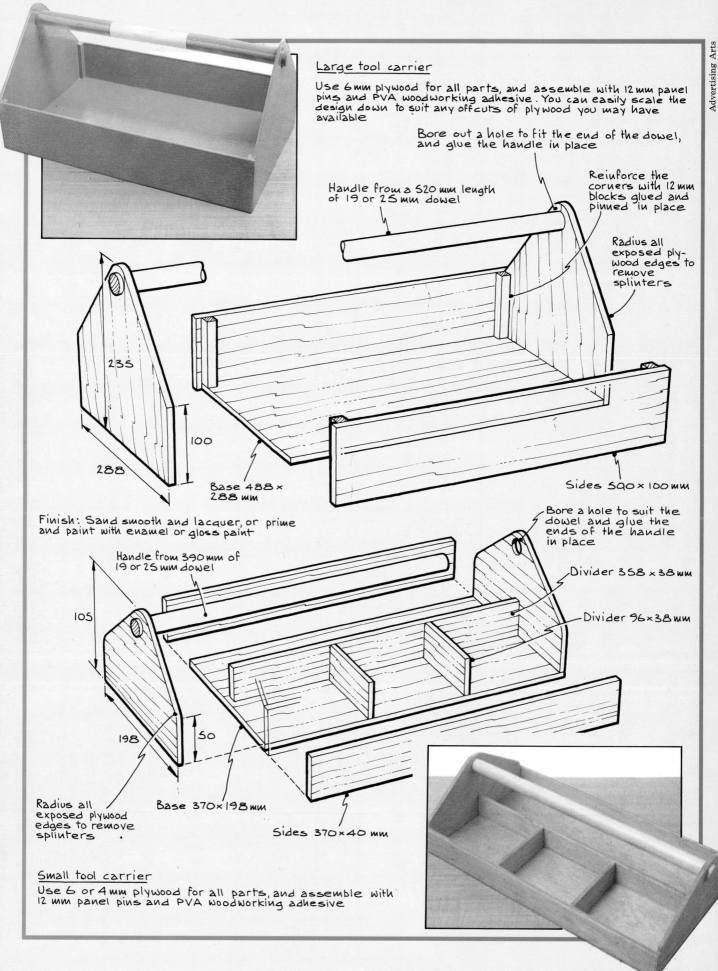

Large tool carrier

Use 6mm plywood for all parts, and assemble with 12mm panel pins and PVA woodworking adhesive. You can easily scale the design down to suit any offcuts of plywood you may have available

Bore out a hole to fit the end of the dowel, and glue the handle in place

Reinforce the corners with 12mm blocks glued and pinned in place

Handle from a 520mm length of 19 or 25mm dowel

Radius all exposed plywood edges to remove splinters

235

100

288

Base 488 × 288mm

Sides 500 × 100mm

Finish: Sand smooth and lacquer, or prime and paint with enamel or gloss paint

Handle from 390mm of 19 or 25mm dowel

Bore a hole to suit the dowel and glue the ends of the handle in place

Divider 358 × 38mm

Divider 96 × 38mm

105

198

50

Radius all exposed plywood edges to remove splinters .

Base 370 × 198mm

Sides 370 × 40 mm

Small tool carrier

Use 6 or 4mm plywood for all parts, and assemble with 12mm panel pins and PVA woodworking adhesive

Dealing with hard water

● The difference between hard and soft water ● The problems of scale and scum ● The benefits of hard water ● Testing for water hardness ● The various treatments for hard water ● Installing a plumbed-in water softener

Water supplied for domestic use is purified to make it bacteria-free—and therefore fit for human consumption—by efficient filtration and storage, as well as by additives and treatments introduced by the water authorities. But even this water contains impurities, in the form of certain amounts of dissolved mineral salts that are referred to when we talk of the *hardness* or *softness* of water.

The concentration of these mineral salts depends largely on the type of rocks and terrain through which the water passes before entering the supply system itself.

What is hard water?

Rainwater which falls in open country and on to insoluble rock such as slate or granite remains more or less mineral-free. Surface water may, however, pick up organic waste products—notably peat which tends to acidify water. This water is usually *soft*.

Conversely, rainwater which falls on to sedimentary rocks tends to permeate through these to emerge as ground water which has a high dissolved mineral content. This water is relatively *hard*.

But there is another side to consider. As rainwater falls to earth it picks up quantities of gases and pollutants which acidify it slightly. The most significant of these acids generally is carbonic acid (soda water), produced by the solution of atmospheric carbon dioxide; but in heavily industrialized areas, with a far greater proportion of sulphur dioxide in the immediate atmosphere, rain can actually fall as a very dilute form of sulphuric acid.

The mildly acid rainwater falls on, and is absorbed by, different rock strata during which time it reacts

A. Right: *Scale is the build-up of particles of the carbonates released from hard water when it is heated. This indirect hot water cylinder shows its serious effects—it was removed from a home after only five years of service*

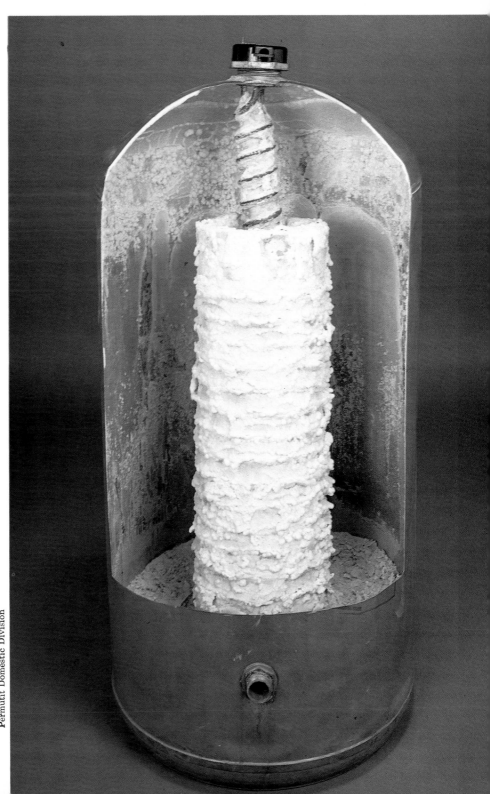

Permutit Domestic Division

with minerals in the rocks themselves. It then either disgorges into rivers, lakes and reservoirs or collects underground and is pumped to the surface.

In regions where there is a high proportion of calcium and magnesium carbonate in the rock—found in limestone and chalky soil, and dolomites respectively—the carbonic acid in the rainwater reacts with the carbonates to produce bicarbonates.

It is these that make the water obviously 'hard' and pose the greatest threat to domestic water systems. At low temperatures, the bicarbonates are readily soluble in water and remain so until they reach your system. But when this water is heated, they begin to decompose into insoluble carbonates which are deposited on any surface at a temperature past the critical point. This is most readily noticeable as 'fur' in a kettle.

Because it can be removed by boiling, such hardness is referred to as *temporary hardness* or *alkaline hardness* and causes the greatest majority

B. Below: *By penetrating clay and limestone, rain can absorb minerals and emerge as hard water*

of problems associated with water quality—heating elements lose their efficiency, and pipes become blocked. Some of the other more stable metal salts which become dissolved in water do increase its corrosive properties and have to be removed for specialist industrial processes. But in domestic installations *non-alkaline hardness*, or *permanent hardness* (which cannot be removed by boiling) is not normally much of a problem. However, sulphate hardness can affect the performance of soaps and detergents—even in areas that do not suffer from carbonate hard water. The addition of a small amount of washing soda reduces this.

Also, all types of water produce a certain amount of corrosion in contact with, for example, the metal of a central heating system. The black sludge you may have noticed after bleeding your radiators is, in fact, the black oxide of iron. Problems of this nature—not directly attributable to water hardness or softness—can usually be cured by adding a corrosion inhibitor to the system (see below).

The problem of scale and scum
Scale is the build-up of particles of the bicarbonates released from hard water

C. Above: *Special crystals encased in a plastic container and suspended in the cold water tank help prevent scale in direct heating systems*

when it is heated. This precipitation begins at around 60°C and accelerates as the temperature is raised. It is for this reason that the first signs of scale are usually found in the kettle, which quickly becomes furred up. Unimportant scale of this sort can usually be removed by boiling up a dilute acid like vinegar or lemon juice together with water. And it can

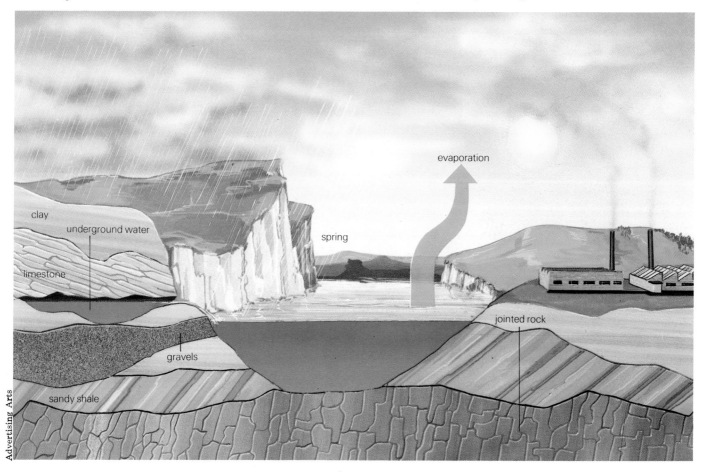

clay

underground water

limestone

spring

evaporation

gravels

sandy shale

jointed rock

Advertising Arts

be prevented from gathering on the heating element by placing a few pebbles in the kettle.

Much more serious is the effect of scale on hot water pipes and central heating systems: pipes become clogged, valves and pumps can jam, and boiler efficiency and life may be drastically reduced. And, as these effects are concentrated at the hottest parts of the system, this is where they can do the most damage.

Washing machines and dishwashers, too, have heating elements which can get covered with scale; this reduces their efficiency because the scale

D. Below: *In a magnetic conditioner, the water flows through a magnetic field. This affects the particles in the water and reduces scale*

has to be heated before—and in addition to—the surrounding water. And of course, electric water heaters are particularly vulnerable to the effects of scale build-up. It has been calculated that boilers having a scale deposit of just 3mm require 15 percent more fuel than scale-free boilers. This figure can rise to a dramatic 70 percent when the scale layer reaches a thickness of 12mm.

Scale formations can cause an objectionable amount of boiler noise—not unlike the creaks, groans and muffled 'explosions' that a furred-up electric kettle makes when heating. But more importantly, unless prevented (or removed, if possible) the scale build-up means a comparatively short life for the appliance and its related pipework.

Scum—insoluble soap curds formed when hard water reacts with soap—is another common problem associated with water containing a high proportion of bicarbonates. It causes unsightly 'tide marks' around baths and sinks, can irritate the skin, and leaves clothes feeling rough to the touch. In fact, twice as much wash powder may be needed for a wash in hard water—and even then, the wash may not be as clean as it would be in soft water areas.

These effects are also seen to a lesser extent with detergents—where china and glassware exhibit faint, but opaque, 'drying marks' for example.

Benefits of hard water
Pure water is tasteless. Hard water, on the other hand, contains dissolved

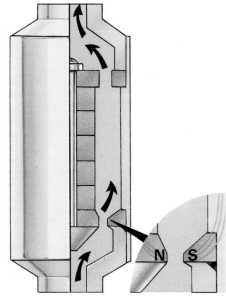

1 *To instal a magnetic conditioner, turn off the water at the main stop-cock, then mark off the section of pipe to be removed*

2 *Remove the pipe section with a fine toothed hacksaw taking care to cut squarely. Have a bucket ready for water left in the pipe*

3 *Assemble the fitting and check that the unit will fit properly. Use compression joints on compact units such as this conditioner*

4 *Slip a backnut and olive over the cut pipe ends. Slide the olives down about 12mm taking care not to damage them*

5 *Then instal the unit, taking care to tighten the backnuts securely. Use a pair of grips—one for holding and the other for tightening*

John Ward

6 *When you have made the joints, assemble the components of the magnetic water conditioner, following the manufacturer's instructions*

John Ward

7 *To maintain the unit, turn off the water and replace the magnet unit with the cap provided. Then turn on the supply again*

traces of many minerals which not only give it flavour but also supply tiny amounts of nutritional elements. Hard water is sometimes recommended for drinking, even though softened water tends to make better coffee and tea. Slight traces of common salt from the softening process (not necessarily detectable by taste) are not tolerated well by most types of garden plant and in any case it is not economical to soften water for this use.

Most domestic water softeners are fitted in such a way as to allow drinking and garden water to bypass the softening system.

Testing your water
The hardness of water varies considerably, even within small geographic regions. If the water is very hard, kettle furring and scummy baths

are a clear sign. But if your soap lathers easily and the water feels soft to the touch, you have soft water.

Your water supply authority should be able to tell you a great deal about the water you receive, and may be able to test any water that comes from a private source not under their specific control. Private firms who instal water softeners may also be able to test the water for you.

Low cost, easy-to-use *water hardness test kits* are readily available from aquarist supply shops. These employ indicator chemicals and you simply count the number of drops needed to effect a colour change in order to obtain a very accurate hardness reading.

Water hardness is measured in several different ways and three systems are in common use. In

scientific circles the measurement is based on parts per million (*ppm*) calcium carbonate—that is, the number of parts of calcium carbonate (CaO_3) present in a million parts of water. The alternative two methods employ a degree system that is indirectly related to the *ppm* system, where hardness is based on parts per million calcium oxide (CaO). One of these systems originated in Germany and is referred to by the symbols DH or °dH. The other is the English system, referred to simply by the degree symbol (°), whose value differs from the DH system.

Confusing as this may seem, the relationship is in fact fairly straight-

E. Below: *Water is diverted from the rising main to the softener and back again. Before installation, do a 'dry run' by assembling the components*

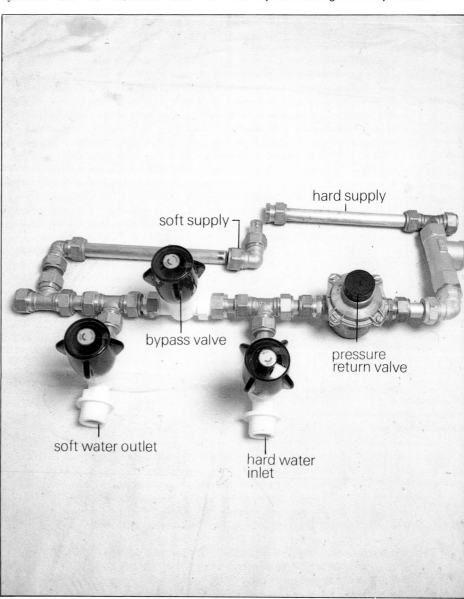

hard supply

soft supply

bypass valve

pressure return valve

soft water outlet

hard water inlet

Nigel Messett

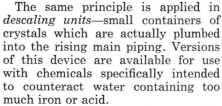

forward. The DH degree is equivalent to approximately 18ppm ($CaCO_3$), the English degree to approximately 14ppm ($CaCO_3$).

Treatments of hard water

A number of possible options exist for the treatment of hard water. Some merely condition it, others actually soften it. The latest development is specifically intended to combat the scale caused by heating.

Chemical scale inhibitors do not actually soften water, but instead stabilize the bicarbonates so that they do not form carbonate scale. Crystals of this type are encased in a plastics container and simply suspended inside the cold water tank which feeds the water heating system (fig. C). This method is cheap but the crystals do need periodic replacement.

The same principle is applied in *descaling units*—small containers of crystals which are actually plumbed into the rising main piping. Versions of this device are available for use with chemicals specifically intended to counteract water containing too much iron or acid.

Corrosion inhibiting solutions can be added directly to indirect heating systems (see pages 26 to 29). Use of these low-cost, non-toxic solutions prevents blockage caused by iron oxide sediment and inhibits the formation of scale. It also prevents the build-up of hydrogen (a by-product of the corrosion process) which is often mistaken for air when bleeding a radiator. Certain special additives help to prevent electrolytic corrosion—often an acute problem in central heating systems.

Most recent of the developments is the *magnetic conditioner* which does not actually change any of the chemical properties of the water, and therefore does not influence its taste and nutritional properties. The conditioner works by passing the water close to strong magnets. These are thought to alter the magnetic properties of the micro-particles enough to dissuade both scale and scum from forming in subsequent pipework and appliances.

Magnetic conditioners have to be matched closely to expected flow rates and require quick maintenance by the householder perhaps twice a year, but are otherwise simply plumbed into a convenient section of the rising main using just two compression fittings (fig. 6). A particular benefit is the small size of the appliance.

8 Before installing the new pipework for a water softener, close the main stopcock to shut off the water supply and drain down

9 The new pipework is inserted into the rising main at a convenient point above the main stopcock. Cut away the old pipework at this point

10 When joining sections of pipework, smear a little jointing compound around the threads of the joints to ensure a watertight seal

11 The new pipe and valve assembly is built up piece by piece and connected, via the non-return valve, to the existing inlet

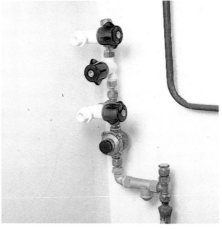
12 Make sure that the cut inlet pipe is capped off. If a separate hard water supply is required, the pipe may be connected later

13 In this installation, water flows to a washing machine through a separate pipe. This is connected to the assembly last

Nigel Messett

14 *Once the assembly is in place, make sure that all three valves are closed, then turn the stopcock back on to renew the water supply*

15 *Waste water flows from this softener through an overflow and a drain hose. Arrange for these to discharge at a suitable drainage point*

16 *With the softener in its correct location, secure the hoses running from it to the overflow and drain with plastic hose clips*

Conditioners do not actually soften the water—for this you need a proper *water softener*. These work by actually removing bicarbonate salts from the water in a process known as ion exchange—the most thorough solution to the problems caused by hard water.

Very simply, ion exchange in a water softener takes place when the electrically-charged bicarbonate ions in the water pass over a catalyst known as the *resin bed*. Here, they change places with ions of sodium and thereafter remain attached to the resin bed while the sodium ions pass harmlessly into the water.

Eventually the resin attracts enough bicarbonate ions to become clogged and it must then be flushed clear with brine solution—which is powerful enough to overwhelm and displace the bicarbonate ions. In all makes of modern water softener this recharging takes place automatically, using salt from a built-in reservoir.

Water softeners are available with different capacities, suited to the amount of water consumed and the hardness locally. There is even a portable model available from one manufacturer. Current advanced models are fairly compact and incorporate automatic timers which open and close valves to control the 'flushing' process or *resin regeneration programme*. They can be timed to do this during the night—when there is no call for water—as two hours or so are required for the regeneration cycle when only hard water is available.

A typical domestic installation requires resin regeneration about twice weekly, using between 1kg and 3kg of salt for the purpose depending on the

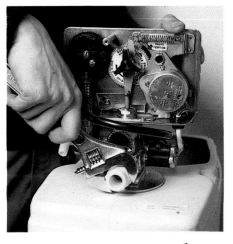

18 *The two hoses which run from the softener to the pipe and valve assembly are joined to the machine by plastic nipple attachments*

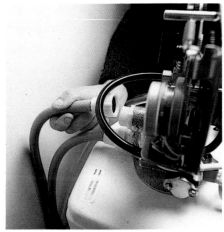

19 *Once the nipples are in place, connect the hoses. The hard water inlet is at the top, with the soft water outlet below*

unit's capacity. The salt reservoir needs topping up every month or two and, apart from occasional servicing, this is the only attention the softener needs. Latest models employ a microchip console to control the valve working the regeneration cycle.

Installing a water softener

The best place to instal a water softener is in a kitchen or laundry room—or wherever the rising main first emerges—but leaving enough pipework for the installation of branch pipes to supply a tap or two for drinking and garden use. The supply will have to be disconnected for at least two or three hours, so lay on supplies of drinking and cooking water before commencing and avoid using any taps in the house except sparingly if there is a water storage tank in the loft.

22 *With the wiring connected, fix the old switch and the cover of the fused spur in place but do not turn on the power at this stage*

Specific instructions vary from make to make, but generally the work entails interrupting the rising main at a convenient point above the main stopcock and then installing inlet and outlet pipes to the softener—the latter rejoining the old rising main to restore a supply link (fig. 14). Between the inlet and outlet pipes, a bypass valve can be located to completely disconnect the softener for maintenance. This is quite separate from the automatically controlled one contained within the softener itself.

Both the inlet and the outlet pipes are usually provided with shut-off valves. But check with your water authorities to see if they require the inclusion of a non-return/air-brake valve. If so, this is located between the inlet valve and the softener.

In areas with particularly high water pressure, you must guard against this exceeding the capabilities of the softener by fitting a pressure reducer between the mains stopcock and the inlet pipe junction. The water softener manufacturers—or the water authority—should be able to advise you whether or not a reducer is considered necessary.

Drain and overflow pipework usually take the form of hosepipes. The drain is often led to a standpipe arrangement incorporating a P-trap, based on the same principle as the drain pipework for a washing machine (see pages) 756 to 760). The overflow pipe is led independently to the outside and it may be necessary to drill and pipe a hole through the wall for this.

Ideally, cut the pipework to individual lengths and lay these in a dry run with fittings loosely arranged to check the plumbing-in arrangement before final assembly. Compression or capillary T-fittings can be used for the inlet and outlet connections to the rising main, though the latter are considerably cheaper. As in all plumbing work, take particular care to ensure that pipes and fittings remain free of dirt and swarf.

Follow specific recommendations for making the electrical connections. Although most units can be connected via a fused plug to an ordinary switched socket, it is better to wire the unit to a fused spur or connection box to prevent accidental switching off (see pages 816 to 823).

After electrical connection, all that remains is to programme and start up the unit—following the manufacturer's specific instructions.

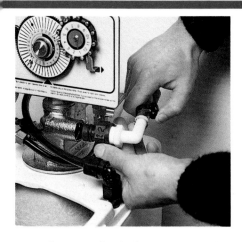

17 Connect the drainage hose to the drainage outlet which is situated below the control mechanism, then connect the overflow hose

20 Connect the hose running from the inlet on the machine to the inlet valve, and the hose from the outlet to the outlet valve above it

21 Having turned off the electricity supply, wire the electric cable from the softener control valve to a fused spur (see pages 818 to 823)

23 Follow the instructions for manual regeneration to flush out the cylinder. Dirty water will flow to the drain for the first few litres

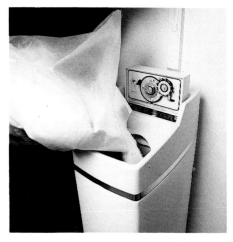

24 Replace the top cover assembly of the softener, then pour granular salt into the filling hole at the top of the machine

25 With the valves open, the unit programmed and the power turned on, the new softener is ready to be tested in operation

Removing a fireplace

● **Types of fireplace surround: tiled, timber, stone, brick and cast-iron** ● **The front hearth and fireback** ● **Planning the work** ● **Removing the surround and hearth** ● **Blocking the opening and making good the fireplace**

An open fireplace with an ugly surround is an unsightly and draughty liability, particularly in a house where fires are rarely lit or central heating has been installed. By removing the hearth and surround and blocking up the opening you can cut expensive heating bills as well as creating a more spacious and attractive room.

However, some old fireplace surrounds—in brick, timber or cast-iron—make an attractive feature which you might not want to destroy, even if you never use the fire. In this case the decorative surround can be retained while the opening is sealed with building blocks or boarding.

Fireplace construction

Most fireplaces consist of a surround, a fireback and grate, and a front hearth. The surround serves a purely decorative function while the fireback, grate and hearth ensure that the fire burns efficiently without risk of accident. Because all of these features vary so much in their construction, it is important to understand how they are built before attempting to demolish and remove them.

Tiled surround: A number of fireplaces, particularly UK ones built in the 1940s and 1950s, consist of a concrete surround and hearth which is then covered in decorative tiles (fig. A). The surround is held in place by two metal plugs, bonded to the concrete backing and screwed firmly into the chimney breast or wall behind the fire.

Timber surround: Many fires have a wooden surround, usually with a stone or concrete front hearth protruding beneath the fire opening (fig. B). The surround is screwed in position on top of a framework of wooden battens fixed to the chimney breast or wall.

Stone or brick surround: This type consists of a number of stone or brickwork courses built up from the hearth against the wall or chimney breast (fig. C). The gap above the fire is often bridged by a 'soldier' arch of bricks placed on end, held up by a steel support underneath. Although stone or brickwork surrounds are usually built without being tied into the wall behind, occasionally steel wall ties—similar to those used in cavity wall construction—are inserted between courses to help strengthen the structure.

Cast-iron surround: These are held in place in a similar fashion to tiled surrounds: plugs bonded to the back of the cast-iron frame are held tight against the wall with screws (fig. D). Most cast-iron surrounds also have an inner cast-iron grate frame fitted around the sides and top of the fireplace and held in position either with nuts and bolts or countersunk screws.

Front hearth: Some fires have a front hearth which protrudes into the room below the fireplace opening and is made of the same material as the surround. This is intended to reduce the risk of hot coals or sparks falling from the grate and accidentally damaging floorings (fig. E).

Fireback: This is a shell-shaped backing made of fireclay which sur-

Left: *Seal the opening neatly using bricks or building blocks. Check that they are correctly aligned with a spirit level or straightedge*

Ray Duns

rounds the grate and prevents damage to the brickwork behind the fire (fig. F).

Planning the work

Removing a fireplace and blocking up the opening is a relatively straightforward job providing you plan the work carefully and have the right tools and equipment to hand.

To remove the surround, hearth and fireback use a crowbar, club hammer and a bolster. These should be adequate for prising the various parts free of their fixings without the need for excessive force, but you will need safety glasses or goggles if you have to hack away mortar with the bolster since loose material is bound to fly.

Where the surround is screwed to the wall or chimney breast you also need a large screwdriver, plus a hacksaw to cut through any fixings which cannot easily be shifted.

Bear in mind that the hearth and surround are likely to prove heavy and you will need the help of at least one other person to dispose of them.

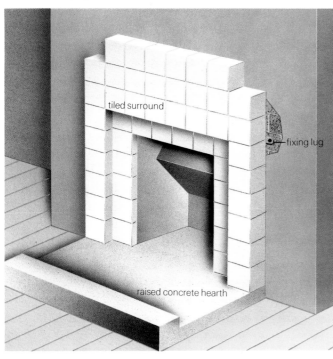

A. Concrete surround covered with tiles

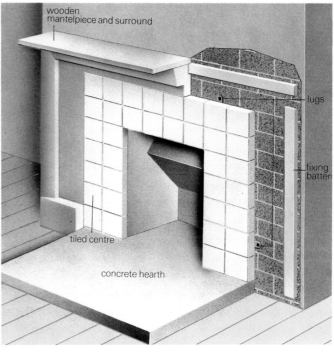

B. Timber surround on wooden battens

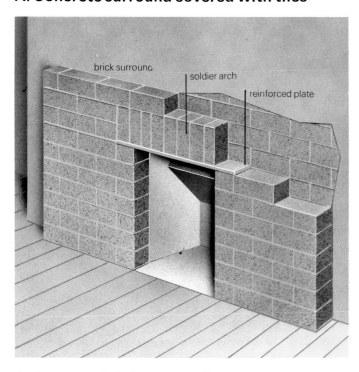

C. Stone or brick surround

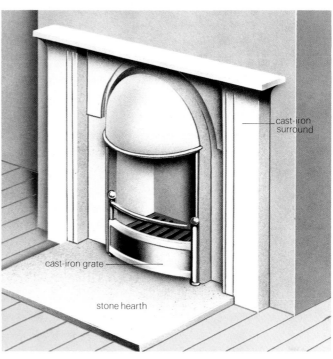

D. Cast-iron surround fixed with plugs

Nigel Osborne

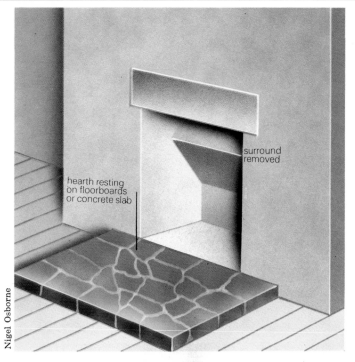

hearth resting
on floorboards
or concrete slab

surround
removed

Nigel Osborne

E. Front hearth construction

F. Shell-shaped fireback

An assistant can also help by steadying the surround while it is being levered free of its fixings.

Once all the equipment has been assembled, clear the room ready for the work. Removing the fireplace will create a great deal of rubble and dust, so it is best to take everything out of the room, including the carpet.

Sheet polythene can be bought in large rolls to completely cover the floor and protect it while the work is going on. If the fireplace is near flat surfaces such as window ledges or built-in furniture, cover these with newspapers and masking tape. A number of heavy-duty polythene bags are useful for disposing of the loose rubble and soot created during demolition and clearance of the site.

Removing the surround

Since the surround is likely to be resting on top of the hearth it is best to start by removing this. The technique you use will depend on how the surround is constructed.

Tiled surrounds: Here the first task is to remove the plaster covering the two fixing lugs. To do this start at the top right hand corner of the fire and chip away the plaster using a hammer and bolster. When you have uncovered the fixing lugs, ask a helper to steady the fire surround while you undo them. Sometimes they will simply unscrew from the wall; if not, cut them off at or near their junction with

the wall using a bolster or hacksaw.

With your helper still steadying the far end of the surround, use your left hand to steady the other end and hold the crowbar in your right hand. Insert this between the surround and the chimney breast, somewhere near the base. If the surround moves by even a few millimetres there are no more fixing lugs. If not, there may be fixing lugs at the bottom edges which should be removed before you proceed.

Once you are sure that all the lugs are free, slowly lower the surround to the ground in front of the fire. Two

people can usually carry the surround outside to be disposed of, but if you have to negotiate a stairway or an awkward doorway, get some extra help.

Removing a timber surround: The procedure used to remove a wooden surround is much the same as for a tiled one except that the fixing lugs usually face towards the fire opening rather than outwards away from it.

Start by taking the crowbar and driving it between the wooden part of the surround and the brickwork behind it. By levering with the crowbar and using your hands to pull the

1 If the fireplace surround has a mantelpiece, start by working this loose with a club hammer and bolster, then lift it clear

2 Remove the plaster down both sides of the surround and, if you uncover the fixing lugs, unscrew or cut them loose

3 *Once the surround has been removed, pull the fireback away from its fixing mortar or break it loose with the club hammer*

4 *The inside of the fireplace is lined with brick. Break this loose with the hammer and bolster and load the material into bags*

5 *Do the same with the bricks along the bottom of the fireplace. Use a small shovel to transfer them to the waste bags*

surround away from the wall you should be able to open a gap between the surround and the wall big enough to look down.

Check whether the timber is held in place by any other fixings—either metal studs or bars. If not, simply lever the facing away from the wall and pull it clear.

If there are other fixings, work your way around the edges of the facing gently levering it away from the wall; do this a small amount at a time to avoid damaging the wall and cracking the brickwork. If the fixings refuse to pull clear, insert a hacksaw between the facing and the wall and cut through the studs or bars.

Removing a brick surround: A stone or brickwork surround is easily removed with a hammer and bolster one course at a time. Starting from the top, insert the bolster into each of the layers of mortar. Then gently tap each brick free and remove it by hand, out of the way.

You may come across steel ties bridging the two walls in which case work these loose by knocking them gently backwards and forwards with the hammer then pull them free with your hand. Continue downwards removing the soldier arch and steel support as you go until you reach the fire hearth.

Levelling the hearth
Most hearths consist of a slab of concrete—usually covered in tiles—which sits below the opening and is bedded into place on a weak lime-mortar mix. If the bottom of the hearth is level with the surrounding floor loosen the bedding mortar by chopping

6 *Then clean the brickwork around the outside of the opening. Remove loose mortar and plaster with a hammer and bolster*

around it with a hammer and bolster. Then insert the crowbar under one end of the hearth and raise it high enough to push a thin batten of wood underneath. Do the same with the other side and you should be able to lift the whole hearth away with the help of another person.

However, if the hearth is lower than the surrounding floor, you have no choice but to break it up or chip it away down to the required level using a hammer and bolster.

Removing the fireback
The fireback is usually held in place by a bed of mortar laid against the edges of the opening. It is usually old and crumbly so if it does not immediately pull free, use the hammer and bolster to break it into more easily handled pieces. The cavity

7 *To help cut down dust, dampen the brickwork behind the opening. A small garden spray makes this job a lot easier and cleaner*

8 *Once the brickwork has been damped down, use a small brush and dustpan to sweep away loose soot and other material*

9 *Fill the opening with bricks or lightweight building blocks. Cut blocks to the correct size with a hammer and bolster*

10 *Lay a thick bed of mortar across the floor just inside the opening. Build upwards, leaving a small gap for the ventilation grille*

11 *As you progress, hold a straight-edge against the face of the blockwork to check vertical and horizontal alignment*

above will be full of soot and rubble and you should make sure that this is removed and the opening brushed clean before you continue.

Blocking up the opening

Once the fireplace has been knocked down and the area cleaned, the opening should be blocked off to prevent draughts and to stop dust falling down the chimney into the room. For this you can use bricks, lightweight building blocks or more lightweight materials such as hardboard, chipboard or asbestos.

In order to bed the blocking material into place and allow a neat plastered finish, you need to cut away some of the existing plaster around the opening with the hammer and bolster. If you decide to retain the present surround, first break out the fireback (see above) and then cut away the plaster around the opening to a distance of about 200mm on each side. Try not to damage the brickwork underneath as you do this and leave straight edges around the area you have cleared away so that final plastering is made easier.

What you do next depends on whether you block up the opening with bricks or some type of sheeting. But whatever method you use, the blocked opening must contain a ventilation grille, fitted at a distance of about 100mm from the floor.

Bricking in: Bricks and lightweight building blocks are both perfectly adequate where you want to block up an opening permanently. But if the opening is particularly small, bricks are preferable since they are easier to manoeuvre and fit into place.

First prepare a mix of 1:4 mortar and lay a bed of it on the floor between the existing wall. Then build up each course of bricks; remember to leave a gap 100mm from the floor to accommodate the vent.

As the wall is built upwards, hold a straightedge against the face of the brickwork to check vertical and horizontal alignment. Any bulges and indentations should be corrected and adjusted before you continue.

Build up successive courses until you fill the cavity. The gap on the last course may be too thin to take whole bricks, so you should cut them lengthways to make up the difference.

Finally, look over the new brickwork and fill all gaps to create a smooth and flat surface. Leave it to dry out for 12 hours before plastering.

Boarding up: For this use 6mm oil-tempered hardboard, chipboard, or if you intend to fit a gas fire in front of the wall, asbestos sheeting. Measure and cut the sheeting to size, and make an internal hole to take the ventilator using a drill and a padsaw. When cutting and drilling asbestos, make sure you wear a mask to avoid breathing in the dust.

Fix the sheeting into place by marking and drilling holes along its edge and using wall plugs to secure it to the wall beneath. If necessary pack it out to bring it nearly level with the surrounding plaster.

Replastering

Before plastering make sure that the surface is prepared properly and that old and flaking plaster is stabilized (see pages 1100 to 1105). Check brickwork for loose mortar: strengthen any

15 *Apply the first coat of plaster in wide, upward sweeps. Push the float hard against the wall to fill deep gaps*

crumbling joints then chip away excess mortar once this has dried. Try to plaster the area neatly by feathering off around the edges (see pages 156 to 159).

Once both coats of plaster have been applied and allowed to dry thoroughly, the ventilation grille can be fitted and fixed firmly in place with bolts or self-tapping screws (fig. 17).

Although the plaster may dry hard after about 20 minutes, it often takes months to settle on the brickwork below; consequently, redecorating—especially with wallpaper—should not be undertaken straight away.

Sealing

Disused fireplaces often run the risk of penetrating damp as a result of rain falling down the chimney. The simplest way of avoiding this is to fit a

12 Once the opening is completely sealed, remove the remaining lengths of skirting board on each side of the chimney breast

13 Damp down all of the brickwork around the opening. This stabilizes the wall and helps the plaster finish to adhere correctly

14 Once the mortar between the blocks has set, run the blade of the bolster along each joint to remove any high spots

16 Finish off with a thin topcoat. Make this as smooth as possible and try to level it off with the existing wall surface

17 Fix the ventilation grille into position using either screws and wall plugs or a thin skim of plaster around the outside

18 When the plaster has dried, cut a piece of skirting board to length and fix it across the front of the chimney breast

rain bonnet—a blocking piece which is cemented into the chimney pot. The bonnet effectively stops rain entering the chimney, but allows air to circulate freely (fig. H).

Alternatively, you could remove the chimney pot, cover the opening with slate and then seal it with mortar flaunching. In this case, though, ventilation must be provided in the form of an airbrick in the chimney stack. The brick should go as high as possible, preferably in the roof space.

Note that in the UK, sealing a chimney constitutes a structural alteration and you will need building permission from your local Building Control office or District Surveyor. He will want to know how the sealed chimney is to be ventilated and also what alternative methods of heating are being used.

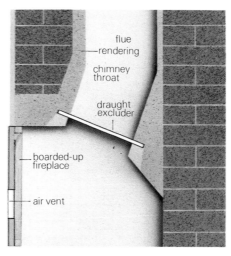

G. Above: Cement a draught excluder across the chimney throat to stop draughts and soot

H. Above: Fit a rain bonnet to the chimney pot. This ventilates the flue, but stops penetrating damp

Nigel Osborne

Exterior door design

The front door to your home is always on show and gives visitors a first impression of your house interior. With very little effort, you can transform your front entrance into a decorative eye-catching feature

Jessica Strang

Bill McLaughlin

Above: *A glazed door can be an important decorative feature, particularly if the glass panels are set in an unusual design and two toning colours are used* **Right**: *Bright colours can make all the difference to the appearance of your front entrance. This deep blue look especially good with white—it picks out the most decorative features and also provides a link with the front gate* **Far right**: *For a more unusual and dramatic finish for a panelled door, paint it plain black, pick out the panel beading in white and apply brightly coloured stencils or or motifs to the centre of each panel as shown here*

The entrance to your home is as much a feature of the exterior appearance of your house as a fireplace, say, is a feature of the living room. And as such its design and decoration should be given just as much consideration. There is a wide range of different types of door furniture from which to choose that will give even the plainest of doors an instant uplift.

It is important to keep the door and door furniture in character with the style of your house. For example, a heavy wooden door can look totally out of place in a modern bungalow, and a simple glazed door too flimsy in a solid-looking brick frontage.

Of course, if you are really unhappy with the style of your door, you can always replace it with an entirely new one. There is a wide range of contemporary styles available as well as a number of reproduction designs.

Solid hardwood doors made from such woods as teak, mahogany or oak can be rather costly—though softwood doors, usually with a deal frame and plywood panels, are less expensive and often look just as good.

Glazed doors look very attractive and are particularly useful for homes which have dark hallways—though they also allow a greater heat loss. It

Elizabeth Whiting

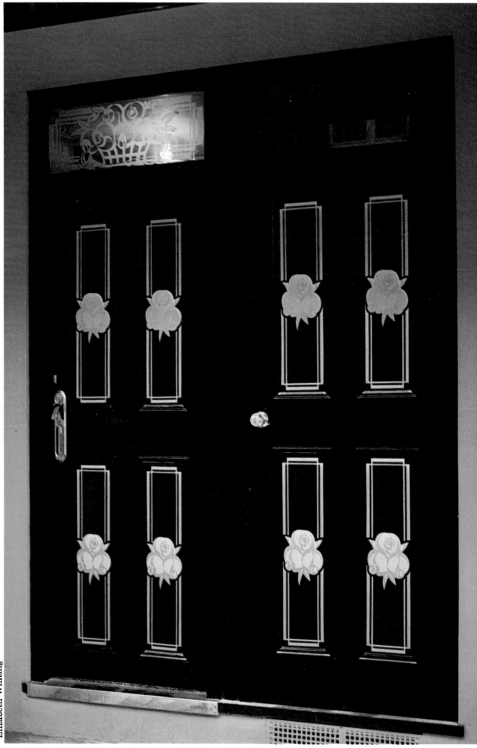

Home designer

is often more practical to instal a glazed panel above the door.

Where your front door is shabby yet basically sound, it might just need a new coat of paint or fresh varnish to give it a new lease of life. You might even prefer the stripped wood finish, once the layers of paint or varnish have been removed.

If your are repainting the door, however, choose a colour that will blend in with the rest of the house or make the door stand out as a feature.

If your front entrance is particularly dark and drab you might consider having something more daring like bright multi-coloured stripes across the door. Or even a simple hand-painted design.

Door furniture

In the same way as doors need to be in character with the exterior appearance of the house, door furniture should complement the style of the door.

Traditionally, door fittings were made from brass, bronze and iron in a wide range of styles. Nowadays these fittings are more likely to be made from chromed or vitreous enamelled steel, zinc alloy or coloured plastics.

Many old doors have brass fittings which are so black with age the brass itself is unrecognizable. But as brass does not rust, it is well worth removing the fittings to give them a thorough cleaning and repolish. To keep them looking rich and sparkling they will need regular care, although you can coat them in a special protective lacquer to avoid the necessity of daily cleaning.

Wherever possible, be sure that the letter box, handle, knocker, keyplate, bell push and so on all match—or at least blend well together. It is often possible to find old pieces in second-hand or antique shops which simply need thorough cleaning—though it might be some time before you manage to build up a matching set.

Antique styles are generally ornate, solid-looking fittings made of black-coated cast-iron. But as it gives a somewhat rural effect, this style is probably best suited to country homes or cottage style houses. Ring pull door knockers make an attractive focal point, and decorative hinges and door studs also improve the overall appearance of the door.

Georgian styles are also ornate, but feature more elegant fitments made from polished brass. This style sets off a plain panelled door beautifully, the knocker becoming the showpiece, and the large door knob a strong feature. One of the most impressive Georgian knockers is the lion's head.

Victorian door furniture is less ornate than Georgian with the urn-shaped knocker as the main feature. Another attractive Victorian-style fitment is the octaganally-shaped centre door knob.

There are, of course, many other styles and designs of fitments, including numbers and house names. The important thing to remember when choosing is that the style of your door and its fittings should make a positive contribution to the exterior appearance of your home.

Below left: *Panelled doors look very attractive when stripped down to the natural wood. Glass panels have been inserted in the top and above the doors for extra light penetration into the hallway* **Below:** *Polished wood looks good on this unusual panelled door which has been finished off with simple brass fittings*

Bill McLaughlin

A concrete planter

Simon Butcher

You can make a planter in any style by using ferro-concrete—and you do not need a mould. Although the technique is quite simple, it takes some practice. But fortunately the materials are very cheap, so you can afford to make several planters.

The basis of the planter is a wire form, which gives it both strength and shape. Make it from lengths of galvanized baling wire and chicken wire mesh. The more wire you use, the stronger the resulting planter, but the harder it will be to pack with mortar. You can make the form in any shape, but the simple flower pot shape shown is the easiest.

Make up a 2:1 mortar mix and add some plasticizer to make it easy to work. Plaster the mould with this, wearing rubber gloves to protect your hands. Work it thoroughly between the wires from both sides. You should aim to build up a 20mm thickness with the form embedded in the centre. It does not matter at this stage if the finish is rough, because you can trim off the excess when the mortar goes 'off' using a trowel, a length of batten or scrapers. The same tools can also be used to add details such as rings or a plinth. Leave a drain hole in the base, then set the assembly aside to allow the mortar to cure. When it is thoroughly dry, fill with earth over gravel.

If you want a more decorative planter, add some colourant to the mortar mix or stain it when dry.

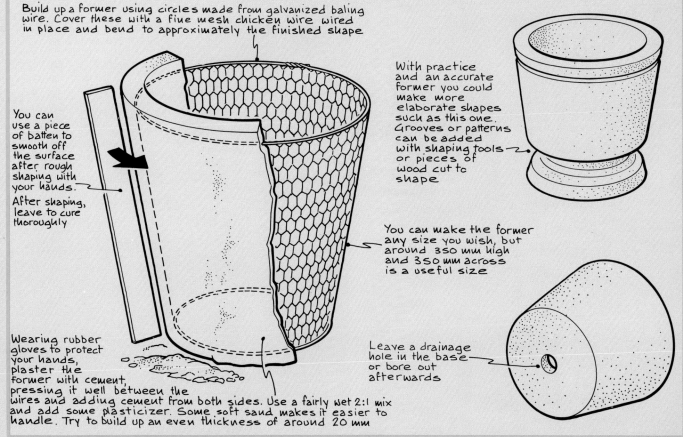

Build up a former using circles made from galvanized baling wire. Cover these with a fine mesh chicken wire wired in place and bend to approximately the finished shape

You can use a piece of batten to smooth off the surface after rough shaping with your hands.

After shaping, leave to cure thoroughly

Wearing rubber gloves to protect your hands, plaster the former with cement, pressing it well between the wires and adding cement from both sides. Use a fairly wet 2:1 mix and add some plasticizer. Some soft sand makes it easier to handle. Try to build up an even thickness of around 20 mm

With practice and an accurate former you could make more elaborate shapes such as this one. Grooves or patterns can be added with shaping tools or pieces of wood cut to shape

You can make the former any size you wish, but around 350 mm high and 350 mm across is a useful size

Leave a drainage hole in the base or bore out afterwards

Advertising Arts

Roofing with PVC sheet

● **The applications of corrugated PVC sheets**
● **Types and sizes** ● **Buying PVC sheet** ● **Hints on working with PVC sheet** ●**Weatherproofing** ● **Sealing with adhesive flashing** ● **How to fix the sheeting to the roof framework**

Transparent or translucent PVC sheets, corrugated to add strength and rigidity, can be used both for roofing and for cladding walls. The material is lightweight, so it is easy to handle. And it is simple to cut, making it ideal for DIY work.

Among the applications to which it is admirably suited are carports, sheds, lean-tos and conservatories. And, although this feature concentrates on using PVC sheeting for roofing, most of the details apply to wall cladding as well.

Types and sizes

The most popular type of sheeting—'75mm round profile'—has smoothly-rounded corrugations with a distance from one 'peak' to another of just under 75mm. Sheeting with squared-off corrugations is also available and again, the distance from the start of one corrugation to the start of the next is about 75mm: this is known as '75mm box profile'.

Some sheets have smaller, rounded corrugations and are known variously as 'mini profile', 38mm, or 32mm

A. *The benefits of PVC roofing are clear for all to see. Where a building demands as much natural light as possible, its light weight and ease of working are distinct advantages*

Gavin Cochrane

profile. These are best suited for wall cladding, or for short roofing spans such as those found on lean-tos. A larger, heavy duty sheet is available for particularly big roofing jobs.

The 75mm profile type usually comes in 760mm wide sheets, measured across the corrugations. Lengths vary from around 1.5m to 3m.

Modern transparent sheeting is very clear and lets through most of the available light, but you can also buy translucent clear and coloured sheets including a semi-transparent white.

Buying PVC sheet

Some brands of sheeting, although clear when they start life, become opaque over the years with the action of sun and rain. If it is particularly important that the sheet remains clear—for example, if you want to use it in a conservatory or greenhouse—make sure you pick a brand that guarantees clarity.

Even clear sheeting varies in its ability to let through light so again, if you are planning a greenhouse, pick a brand that lets through the maximum amount.

When you are selecting sheets, check that they are not split, damaged, discoloured, or distorted. When you get them home, stack them flat—on battens and covered with a tarpaulin, if they are left outside. Although you should never stack it in direct sunlight, cold weather makes PVC brittle and it is a good idea to leave the sheets in a warm room for a day before cutting.

When you are calculating quantities assume each sheet covers about 10 percent less than its actual area to allow for the overlap at the sides with adjoining sheets.

At the same time, buy a supply of purpose-made fixing screws, allowing roughly 25 for each square metre of roof area.

Round-head chrome plated screws, 45mm long, are the best for roofing work. Special plastic caps and washers are needed to waterproof the holes through which they go, so it is sensible to buy a supply of the fixing accessory packs that are sold for use with the sheeting; indeed, if you do not, you may lose the benefit of any guarantee you get.

The structure which supports the sheet is normally timber and often ends up more complicated and costly than the covering itself. Choose only well-seasoned timber and make sure that it is adequately preserved before you fit it (see pages 841 to 847). Bear in mind that you may need flashing materials to seal a joint between the sheet and an existing wall (see pages 1364 to 1368).

Working with PVC sheet

PVC sheeting is quite easy to cut and drill, providing you follow some simple rules. It can be marked for both with a felt-tip pen and obtrusive marks may be removed by rubbing with a cloth soaked in methylated spirit. One handy hint which aids marking out is to cut a strip of the material and use this as a template for all further cutting (fig. 3).

Cutting is best done with a tenon saw or fine-toothed panel saw, though for cutting off small pieces you could try tinsnips or a pair of heavy scissors. Cut at a shallow angle, and support

1 Start by measuring the distance between the lower wall or fascia (if fitted) and the wall plate on the house wall

2 Transfer your measurement to the PVC sheet, allowing roughly 150mm extra for a sufficient amount of overlap at the eaves

3 Cut a strip of the PVC sheet and use it as a template to mark cutting lines on the rest of the sheet in felt-tip pen

4 Before you cut PVC sheeting, you must support it on both sides of the cutting line and cramp it securely in position using wood offcuts

5 Cut the PVC sheet at a shallow angle using a fine toothed panel saw or a tenon saw. Beware of trying to apply too much pressure

Gavin Cochrane

the sheet carefully on both sides of the line down which you are cutting (fig. 4). In cold weather it is best to cut indoors—and handle the sheeting especially carefully.

Holes for the fixing screws should be drilled slightly larger than the diameter of the screw shank to allow the sheet to expand freely. With the type of screws usually used for roofing,

a 7mm hole—giving a clearance of about 3mm—is ideal.

Support the sheet on the opposite side to which you are drilling the hole and do not allow it to bow under pressure. Both hand and power operated drills can be used, together with ordinary twist bits, but you may find that a slightly blunt bit makes a cleaner hole than a new one.

Make larger diameter holes by drilling a circle of tiny holes—say 3mm diameter—and then joining these up with a fine padsaw blade. In this case increase the clearance for expansion to around 4–5mm.

Supporting PVC sheet

The corrugations on PVC sheet give it some degree of rigidity, but it still needs to be well supported if it is not to fly off in the first high wind.

The main supports are *purlins*—the timbers which run at right-angles to the direction of the corrugations in the sheet (fig. B). These should be set no more than 600mm apart—so a sheet 1.8m long must be supported top and bottom and by two inbetween.

The purlins, which generally measure 25mm or 38mm in width, are in turn supported by rafters running at right-angles to them along the direc-

B. *One way to fix the PVC sheets to the fascia is with battens (A). To ensure complete weatherproofing (B) you must use the PVC washers and screw caps with every screw*

An alternative method of securing the sheets to the fascia (C) is to 'spring' the edge into a groove cut in the board. Eaves filler strip (D) offers a seal at the eaves

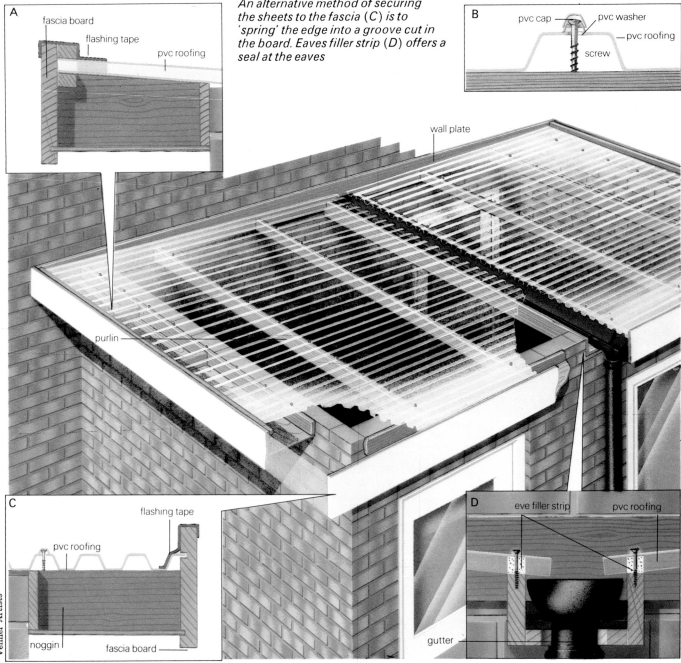

A
fascia board
flashing tape
pvc roofing

B
pvc cap pvc washer
pvc roofing
screw

wall plate

purlin

C
flashing tape
pvc roofing
noggin fascia board

D
eve filler strip pvc roofing
gutter

Venner Artists

tion of the corrugations. The distance between rafters depends on the depth of the purlins as given below:

Depth of purlin timber (mm)	Space between rafters (m)
75	1.6
100	2.2
125	2.7
150	3.2
175	3.8
200	4.3
225	4.8

It can be seen that if your structure is small enough, and you use thick enough purlins, you will not need any intervening rafters: the purlins can be

supported on whatever forms the ends of the structure. For example, purlins 38mm wide by 100mm deep will span a structure 2.2m wide without additional support. The size of the rafters too, depends on the width that they have to span—timber 38mm wide and 100mm deep should span up to about 3m.

It is likely that the structure you want to build will not be free-standing but a lean-to, using a house wall for support. In this case, the roof usually slopes away from the house and the final purlin is supported on a wall plate, plugged and screwed to the

house wall. If the structure has no rafters, 75mm × 25mm timber should be suitable. If the structure has rafters, the wall plate will usually support their ends, and 75mm × 50mm timber would be best. One method of fixing rafters to the wall plate is shown in (fig. C); note that the gap between the wall and the plate itself must be well sealed with mastic.

C. A snowguard (left) is essential to prevent tiles from falling on to the roofing. To seal the roof-to-fascia board join (A) fix the edge of the sheet into a bed of mastic

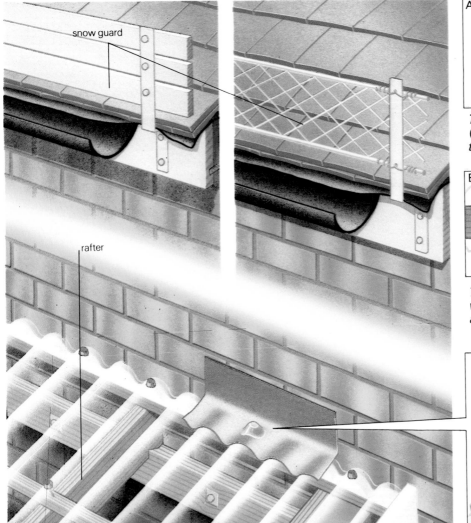

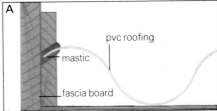

To double glaze with PVC sheeting (B) fix a second layer of sheeting to the underside of the purlins

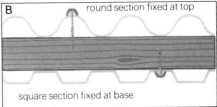

To efficiently weatherproof the wall/roof join (C) use a bed of mastic and adhesive flashing tape

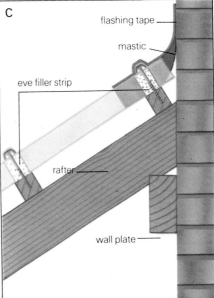

Gavin Cochrane

6 Before fixing any flashing tape to the wall, you should paint a coat of bitumen primer on the contact surface to stabilize it

7 Unroll a manageable length of adhesive flashing tape, lay it in position, and form an L shape leaving the lower flap free

8 Smooth out wrinkles in the tape with a block of waste softwood, and flatten the edges so that water cannot penetrate

Weatherproofing

The easiest way of ensuring that a simple structure is reasonably weathertight is to allow the sheets to overhang it all the way round. The amount of overhang at the bottom of the slope depends on whether you want guttering: if you do, arrange the overhang so that rainwater will flow properly in to the gutter; if not, have a larger overhang so that the rain is thrown clear of the base. An overhang of 250mm would not be too large.

For a more airtight structure, the top and bottom can be filled with *eaves filler strip* (fig. 11)—foam strip in the shape of the corrugations. The strips should be placed on the supporting timbers before the sheets are fixed in place and the fixing screws driven through them. Hold the strip in place as you insert the screws.

Overhanging sheet looks unattractive if left by itself so for a neater appearance, fix fascia boards all round—whether you are fitting guttering or not. The fascias are best fixed directly to the purlins or rafters, so arrange for these to overhang the structure by a suitable amount.

Whatever the size of your roof design, you should make sure there is a slight fall towards the gutter edge and along the corrugations, not across them. A fall of 10° or more is preferable although much steeper slopes can be used if you want.

Try to co-ordinate your design and the sheet sizes so that you do not have to join sheets end to end. Alternatively, redesign the structure to suit—for example by turning the slope through 90°, or siting the gutter in the middle of the span, rather than along

9 Drill slightly into the purlins or rafters supporting the sheets, then insert the fixing screws and their PVC washers

one edge. If you do have to join sheets end to end, they must be overlapped by at least 150mm with a purlin below.

Flashing

There are two main methods of sealing the joint between the sheet and a house wall. The easiest is to use proprietary, flexible, self-adhesive flashing strip in conjunction with its own bituminous surface primer. This is easy to apply, and is pliable enough to fold into the corrugations.

An alternative method where the corrugations are to run at right-angles to the wall is shown in fig. C. Here, you lay the sheets half way up the final purlin—which should be wider than the rest—then fill out the rest of it with strips of packing timber the height of the corrugations. You then

10 Tighten the screws so that the sheet is held securely without distorting, then clip the special PVC screw covers in place

12 To ensure a draughtproof seal you can lay a strip of preformed eaves filler along the top of the wall, and screw through it

lay a final timber strip the same width as the purlin over the sheet ends and the packing. Push this up against the house wall and secure it by nailing through the packing to the purlin. Seal the gap between the wall and the strip by packing it with a suitable mastic. The same technique can be used to form a pitched roof ridge.

Where the corrugations run parallel to the house wall, a wall plate carries the ends of purlins rather than rafters, and the fixing and sealing arrangements are a little different.

Round profile sheet can be sealed to the wall plate with bevelled timber packing pieces—one above the sheet, and the other below. Bed in the edge of the sheet with mastic. The technique can be used with box profile sheet too, but a neater method is to cut a groove in the wall plate with

a circular saw, and to 'spring' the edge of the sheet into this. Remember to cut the groove at the same angle as the roof slope and again, bed in the sheet ends with mastic (fig. B).

Double glazing

Heat loss through PVC sheet is very high, and this makes it unsuitable for use as a permanent room. However, some of the heat loss can be reduced by 'double glazing'—fixing another layer of sheeting to the underside of the supporting purlins.

In this case, weatherproofing is unnecessary and you can fix the sheet in its valleys, using shorter screws. However, it is important to seal both exterior and interior layers, so that the air in the cavity is still. Use eaves filler strip at the edges, and overlap joints in the same way as for the exterior layer. If there are rafters in the construction, cut the sheet to fit between them and seal the joints between the two as shown in fig. 12.

It is essential that both interior and exterior layers are of the clearest sheet you can get—less transparent sheets may lead to a build up of heat in the cavity, causing them to warp.

Fixing the sheet

When you come to fix the sheets to the supporting structure, you may find yourself doing more than one job at once. For example, it would be better to fit self-adhesive flashing as you go along rather than leave it to the end and risk falling through the roof. And, if you are sealing joints, have the necessary materials to hand before you start overlapping.

On a roof, the idea is to have the joint overlaps running away from any

prevailing winds, with the slope. You must bear this in mind when you choose which end to start sheeting; and if sheets are to be joined end to end, fix the bottom row first.

Lay the first sheet at right-angles to the supporting purlins, at one end of the structure.

Drill screw holes through the first corrugation on the non-jointed side to both end rafters and all purlins; on a standard, 1.8m long sheet this should mean at least four fixings. Note that the holes should run through the crest of the corrugation.

You may find that there is not enough support beneath a crest for you to drill without distorting the sheet. In this case, mark the positions of all the fixing holes and turn the sheet over—you will find that the crests have become valleys, and are easy to drill through. After drilling turn the sheet back again and fix through the first corrugation, taking care not to overtighten.

Continue in this way along the sheet, drilling and screwing at every third corrugation, but do not yet fasten the last corrugation.

Now lay the next sheet on the structure, lap its first corrugation over the last corrugation of the preceeding sheet, and fasten the two together. Repeat the process for subsequent sheets, if necessary completing any sealing and fastening work as you go.

If there is to be an upper layer of sheeting, it must overlap the other by at least 150mm—and by twice as much if the roof slope is less than 10°. You must remove the topmost row of fixings on the lower sheets before fixing the upper ones in place.

11 *Clip PVC caps over the screw heads in order to seal up the holes and prevent water from leaking through the roof*

13 *Seal the overlap between each sheet with the special adhesive tape supplied by the manufacturer for this purpose*

14 *Finally seal the gap between the wall and the roofing sheet with the adhesive flashing tape, pressing it firmly into place*

15 *To assemble the snowguard, first screw the support brackets to the fascia board then secure the wire guard to them*

A bedside cabinet

Make this attractive cabinet as a useful piece of bedside furniture. The simple design is easy to build, and you can adapt it in many ways to suit your own requirements

This practical bedside cabinet is a simple box construction in veneered chipboard. You can build it as shown here with three drawers for maximum storage, or omit one or more drawers and fit shelves or a cupboard door.

The example in the picture is made from pine veneered chipboard, but you can use different veneers or even paint it to match the colours of your decorative scheme.

Whichever way you want to build it,

the main carcase is the same. If you are fitting a shelf, do so when you assemble the carcase.

All the drawers are made in the same way, by grooving and housing the chipboard sides.

Finish all the cut edges with iron-on edging strip to match the veneer, and sand down thoroughly. Finish with lacquer or paint as you require, then fit the handles or drawer pulls of your choice to suit the finish.

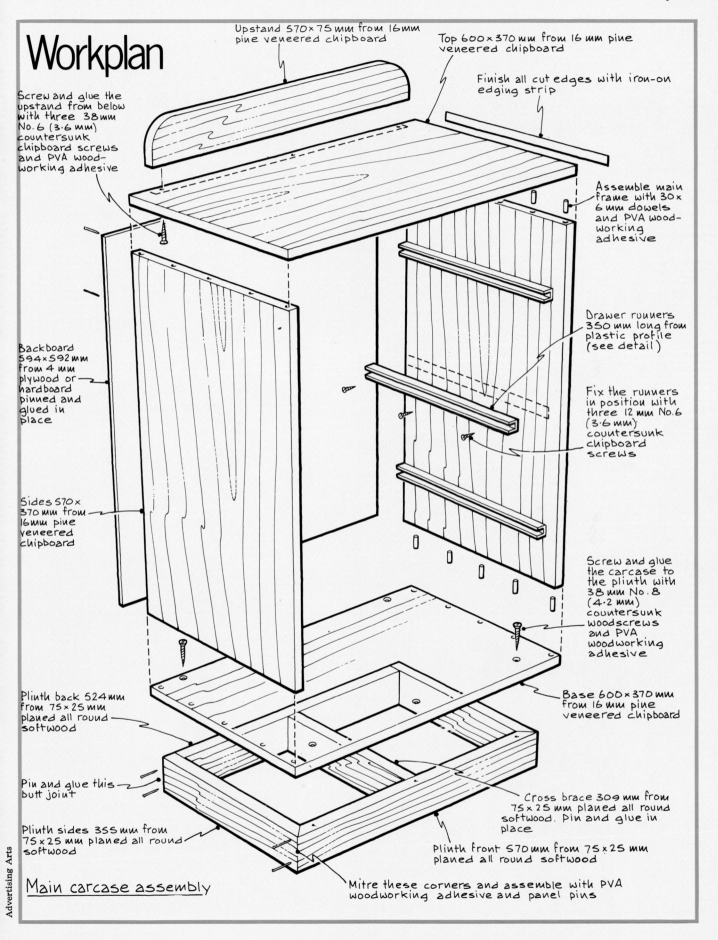

Workplan

Upstand 570×75 mm from 16mm pine veneered chipboard

Top 600×370 mm from 16 mm pine veneered chipboard

Finish all cut edges with iron-on edging strip

Screw and glue the upstand from below with three 38mm No. 6 (3·6 mm) countersunk chipboard screws and PVA wood-working adhesive

Assemble main frame with 30× 6 mm dowels and PVA wood-working adhesive

Backboard 594×592mm from 4 mm plywood or hardboard pinned and glued in place

Drawer runners 350 mm long from plastic profile (see detail)

Fix the runners in position with three 12 mm No.6 (3·6 mm) countersunk chipboard screws

Sides 570× 370 mm from 16mm pine veneered chipboard

Screw and glue the carcase to the plinth with 38 mm No. 8 (4·2 mm) countersunk woodscrews and PVA woodworking adhesive

Plinth back 524mm from 75×25 mm planed all round softwood

Base 600×370 mm from 16 mm pine veneered chipboard

Pin and glue this butt joint

Cross brace 309 mm from 75×25 mm planed all round softwood. Pin and glue in place

Plinth sides 355 mm from 75×25 mm planed all round softwood

Plinth front 570 mm from 75×25 mm planed all round softwood

Mitre these corners and assemble with PVA woodworking adhesive and panel pins

Main carcase assembly

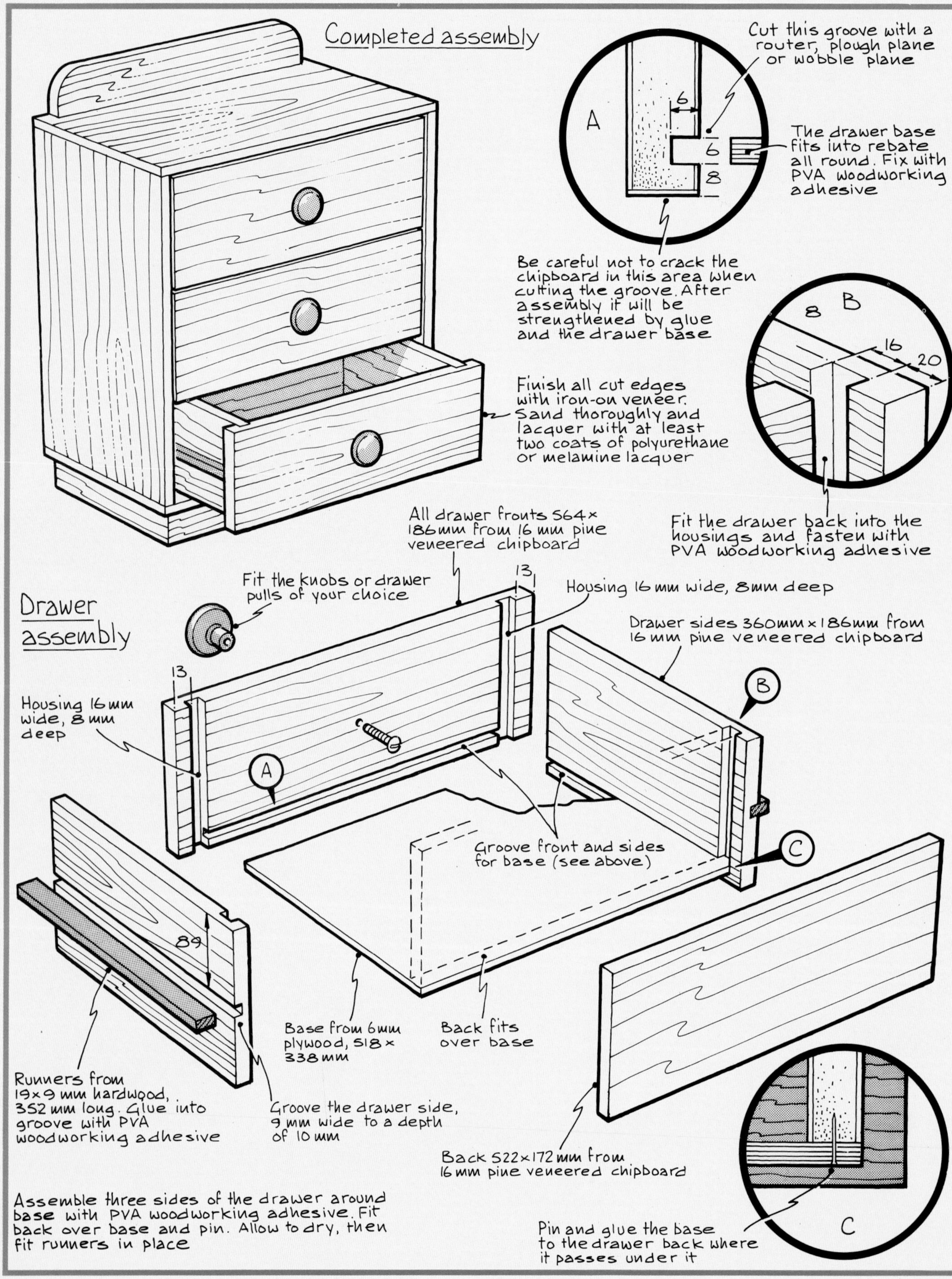

Project

Completed assembly

Cut this groove with a router, plough plane or wobble plane

A

6

6

8

The drawer base fits into rebate all round. Fix with PVA woodworking adhesive

Be careful not to crack the chipboard in this area when cutting the groove. After assembly it will be strengthened by glue and the drawer base

8   B

16

20

Finish all cut edges with iron-on veneer. Sand thoroughly and lacquer with at least two coats of polyurethane or melamine lacquer

Fit the drawer back into the housings and fasten with PVA woodworking adhesive

Drawer assembly

Fit the knobs or drawer pulls of your choice

All drawer fronts 564 × 186mm from 16 mm pine veneered chipboard

13

13

Housing 16 mm wide, 8mm deep

Drawer sides 360mm × 186mm from 16mm pine veneered chipboard

B

Housing 16 mm wide, 8 mm deep

A

C

Groove front and sides for base (see above)

89

Base from 6mm plywood, 518 × 338mm

Back fits over base

Runners from 19 × 9 mm hardwood, 352 mm long. Glue into groove with PVA woodworking adhesive

Groove the drawer side, 9 mm wide to a depth of 10 mm

Back 522×172 mm from 16 mm pine veneered chipboard

C

Assemble three sides of the drawer around base with PVA woodworking adhesive. Fit back over base and pin. Allow to dry, then fit runners in place

Pin and glue the base to the drawer back where it passes under it

Cutting list

All sizes are in millimetres. Chipboard is 16mm pine veneered.

Part	Material	No.	Size
top bottom	16mm chipboard	2	600×370mm
sides	16mm chipboard	2	570×370mm
plinth front	75×25mm softwood	1	570mm
plinth back	75×25mm softwood	1	524mm
plinth sides	75×25mm softwood	2	355mm
plinth brace	75×25mm softwood	1	309mm
back	4mm ply or hardboard	1	594×592mm
drawer fronts	16mm chipboard	3	564×186mm
drawer sides	16mm chipboard	6	360×186mm
drawer backs	16mm chipboard	3	522×172mm
drawer bases	6mm plywood	3	518×338mm
drawer runners	19×9mm hardwood	6	352mm
frame runners	plastic profile	6	350mm
upstand	16mm chipboard	1	570×75mm
shelf (optional)	16mm chipboard	1	568×370mm
door (optional)	16mm chipboard	1	565×378mm

Additional materials: drawer pulls, chipboard screws, woodscrews, PVA woodworking adhesive, panel pins, edging veneer
Finish: polyurethane or melamine lacquer

Cross section of cabinet

Set the drawer runners at these spacings

90

190

190

Front view of cabinet

174

Remember to allow for the thickness of edging veneer when joining these corners

Inset the plinth 15mm from the front

Chamfer the edges of the back panel

If you prefer, you can adapt the basic design to have an open void over a shelf instead of the top drawer. Omit the top drawer, and when you are assembling the carcase, dowel joint a further chipboard panel in place. The dimensions of the shelf are 568×370mm from 16mm pine veneered chipboard

A

Inset the plinth 15mm from each side

This drawing shows details of the drawer runner assembly. The hardwood section fitted to the drawer bears on a plastic profile fitted to the side. Smooth of the wood thoroughly and wax to ensure a smooth running drawer

Drawer side

Round these edges slightly

Side panel

A

Hardwood runner

Plastic drawer runner profile

Martin Palmer

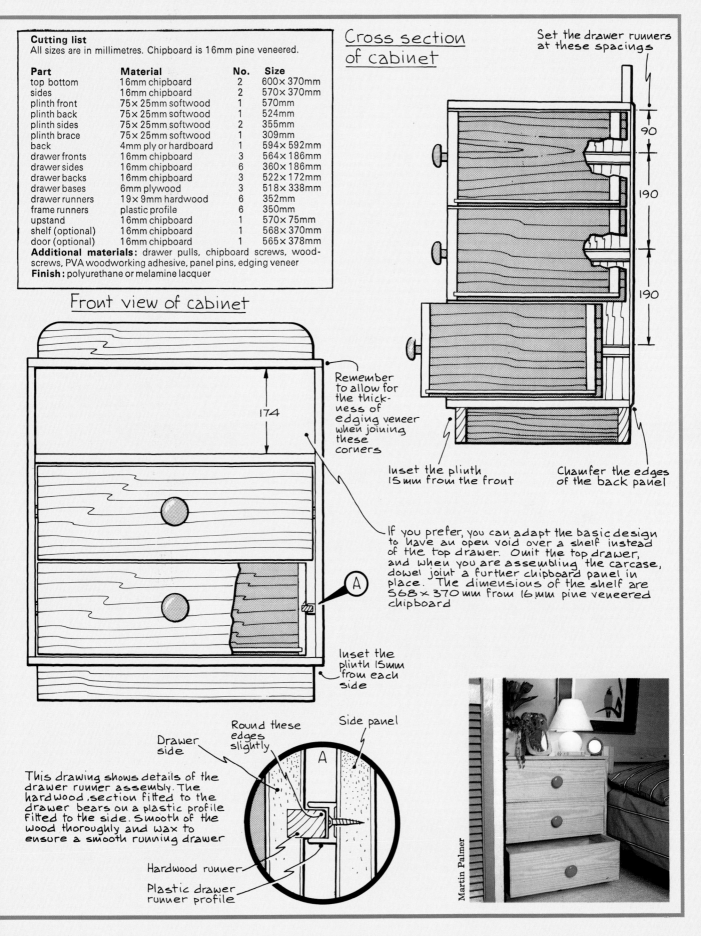

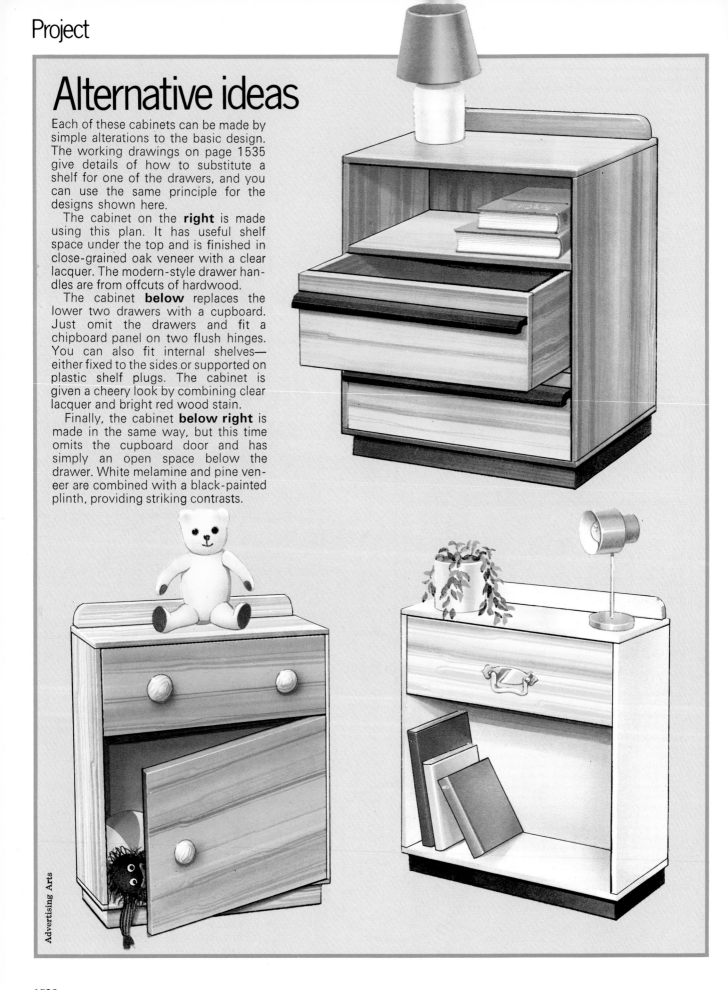

Alternative ideas

Each of these cabinets can be made by simple alterations to the basic design. The working drawings on page 1535 give details of how to substitute a shelf for one of the drawers, and you can use the same principle for the designs shown here.

The cabinet on the **right** is made using this plan. It has useful shelf space under the top and is finished in close-grained oak veneer with a clear lacquer. The modern-style drawer handles are from offcuts of hardwood.

The cabinet **below** replaces the lower two drawers with a cupboard. Just omit the drawers and fit a chipboard panel on two flush hinges. You can also fit internal shelves— either fixed to the sides or supported on plastic shelf plugs. The cabinet is given a cheery look by combining clear lacquer and bright red wood stain.

Finally, the cabinet **below right** is made in the same way, but this time omits the cupboard door and has simply an open space below the drawer. White melamine and pine veneer are combined with a black-painted plinth, providing striking contrasts.

Advertising Arts

More door repairs

● **Different types of door** ● **Internal and external door frame construction** ● **Common door problems** ● **Removing and straightening warped doors** ● **Altering a door frame** ● **Repairing and replacing damaged door frames**

Simon Butcher

Warped or damaged doors need not necessarily be scrapped: very often you can save money by carrying out your own repairs to the door itself, or by modifying the frame or door stops to accommodate the damage

Doors and door frames are as susceptible to damage as any other part of the woodwork in your house. And although you can buy new doors and frames 'off the peg' to replace rotten or damaged ones, you can save yourself a great deal of money by carrying out simpler repairs and maintenance before it is too late.

Pages 705 to 709 describe some of the steps you can take to rectify simple door problems, while pages 1453 to 1459 deal with the specific problems found on traditional, side-hinged garage doors. Re-read these pages before you start work.

Types of door

There are three basic types of door: the *ledged and boarded* door; the *panelled* door; and the *flush panelled* door. Standard sizes of most types are available, but remember that interior doors are usually narrower and thinner than exterior doors.

Softwood is the most common construction material, although hardwood, metal and plastic are also used.

Ledged and boarded doors: These are made from vertical tongued-and-grooved boards, nailed to horizontal ledges and diagonally braced.

1 *This door will not close properly because it is warped—the stile is bent and the door sticks out slightly at the bottom*

1537

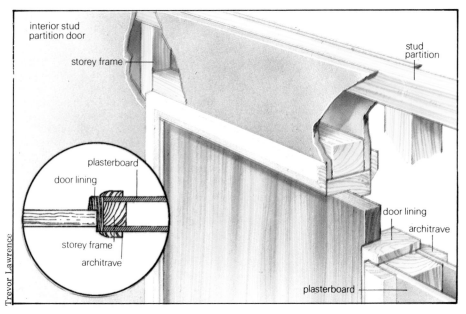

Trevor Lawrence

A. *The simplest door frame of all—a doorway in a stud partition wall. Removal and replacement of this kind of door frame is comparatively easy*

The diagonal members resist the tendency to sag, and a stronger version has vertical stiles on the shutting edges to which the ledges are attached. Most locks can be fitted to this type of door, although the diagonal braces must be retained to resist sagging and warping.

Panelled doors: These have a solid frame made up from vertical stiles and horizontal rails which enclose the panels. The panels can be made from plywood or glass, and are usually fixed by mouldings running around the inside of the frames. One side of the panel fits into a rebate and butts against the moulded edges of the stile and rail; a matching bead is pinned and glued to the other side of the panel to hold it in place.

Panelled doors are available in a variety of sizes, and you can plane the edges to suit the size and shape of your opening.

Flush panelled doors: These usually consist of an internal wooden frame to which a plywood or hardboard facing is pinned. Between the two facings you will often find insulating or fire-resistant material—although some exterior doors are solid.

Because the facing panels help to prevent the door sagging, the stiles and rails are often very narrow. When you buy a new door, therefore, make sure that it is as near the same size as the frame as possible or you may run out of timber to plane off the edges.

Some flush panelled doors have a plasticized coat on the facing for use

in bathrooms and if you must plane a door like this, protect the coat by lining the edges with masking tape. Afterwards you can protect the bare timber with polyurethane lacquer.

Doorways and linings

Doors need doorways, and it is very often the door frame rather than the door which requires your attention. Again there are three basic types, each one intended for a different type of wall construction.

The simplest type of frame construction—used in stud partition walls—consists of lining boards at the top and on each side of the opening. These can be bolted, screwed, or nailed to the wall studs (fig. A).

A similar construction is used for doorways in brick partition walls, though in this case the lining is often attached to a timber *ground* which is fixed directly to the brickwork. The ground and/or lining may be fixed to the wall with screws and plugs, with fixing cramps, or with screws driven into wooden blocks set into the brickwork itself (fig. B).

If you need to, you can find out exactly how the frame is fixed by prising off one of the vertical architraves, chipping away the plaster, and looking in the gap between the lining and the surrounding masonry.

Either of the above types of construction can use rebated or planted stops and both are surrounded by wooden architraves.

The architrave is simply a timber moulding which is nailed over the joint between the wall plaster and the doorway lining to conceal the gap. It is usually pinned to the lining with a mitred joint at the top corners, and

2 *To correct this, nail a block of wood to the door stop where this first makes contact with the door when the latter is shut*

4 *Nail a wooden batten to the block that is long enough to wedge the door shut, but can be swung out of the way when you want to open it*

Simon Butcher

6 *The catch will not only hold the top of the door firm—if the top of the door is warped it makes an equally good corrective wedge*

3 *Next open the door and nail a block of timber to the floor so that it does not foul the door when this is opened and shut in normal use*

5 *To prevent the top of the door moving out, screw a wooden catch to the door frame which can be swung out of the way when required*

7 *If you want to modify the doorstop, begin by planing a piece of timber to the same thickness as the gap between door and stop*

can easily be prised away undamaged. Should you need to do this, knock out the old nails and refix it with new nailing, then fill the old nail holes with putty before repainting.

Exterior doorways are slightly different. Here a hardwood sill is usually an integral part of the frame, which is itself fitted directly into the opening and is secured to the surrounding masonry by galvanized steel fixing cramps. The cramps and door frame are fixed into the wall as the brickwork is erected (see pages 713 to 716). Sometimes the *horns* of the frame-ends which project horizontally from the top of the main frame are also built into the wall (fig. C).

Exterior door frames are much more likely to suffer from wet rot than interior ones, so on most door frames the gap between the frame and the wall is sealed with non-hardening mastic to prevent moisture getting in and attacking the frame from behind. For the same reason, the gap should also contain a vertical damp-proof course of PVC or bituminous felt.

Sticking doors

Sticking doors can be caused by sagging joints in the door itself, by sticking hinges, or by a damaged door frame. Planing the edges of the door or resetting the hinges may cure minor problems, but to repair bad cases you will have to completely dismantle and refurbish the door and its joints, and/or the door frame (see pages 705 to 709, and 1453 to 1457).

B. *An interior doorway in a brick partition wall—structurally stronger than a stud partition door frame but more trouble to replace*

Twisted or warped doors

Panelled and ledged and boarded doors are prone to twisting and warping. When this happens, the door does not close properly and the lock and latch often mismatch.

Unfortunately, in the case of ledged and boarded doors there is not much you can do to rectify this other than complete refurbishment or replacement. You could try replacing the most badly twisted boards, or screw a couple of sturdy ledges to the exterior face of the door, but this is not always successful.

Panelled doors are as difficult to rectify, but your chances of success are higher. However, if the door is glazed, remove the glass before trying to carry out any work.

The first solution to try is forcing the door against its twist. Close the door until it just touches the doorstop, then measure the gap where the door does not touch. Cut and shape a wooden block slightly larger than this gap and fit it between the door and the stop at the point where they first touch. Force the door shut along its length, wedging it firmly in place for two or three days while the house is empty during the day and at night.

A method that is more likely to succeed involves a good deal more work. Remove the door and place it on a bench with the side towards which the stile twists facing upwards. Remove the nailed beading on this side and with a tenon saw make a number of saw cuts across the stile in the area where the curve is greatest, cutting halfway through it. Cramp the door to the bench to pull it flat.

Next mark cutting lines for notches 25–40mm wide either side of the saw

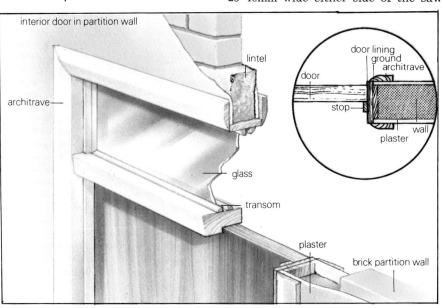

interior door in partition wall

architrave

lintel

glass

transom

plaster

brick partition wall

door lining
ground
architrave
door
stop
wall
plaster

Repairs and renovations

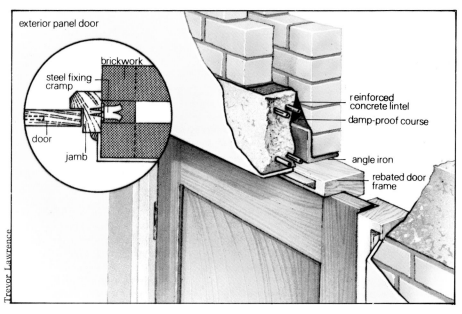

exterior panel door

brickwork

steel fixing cramp

door

jamb

reinforced concrete lintel

damp-proof course

angle iron

rebated door frame

Trevor Lawrence

8 *Use the timber as a gauge to mark out the new line of the doorstop by running it down the shut door with a soft pencil or scribe*

12 *Check that the two stops are the same thickness at the corner where they meet, then nail them back into position on the frame*

C. *An external frame fitted in a cavity wall. Damp-proofing and structural strength are vitally important in an external door frame*

cuts. The notches should taper slightly as shown in fig. D with the narrow ends nearest the centre of the door. Follow by marking the depths of the notches—which should be no more than a third the thickness of the stile—on the edges of the stile. Use a sliding bevel to make the edges of the cut-out slightly undercut like a dove-tailed joint (fig. D). Then remove the waste with a tenon saw and a bevel edged chisel.

Cut softwood wedges to fit each cut-out, making them slightly longer than the width of the stile and with the grain running in the same direction. Tap the wedges into the cut-outs and release the cramps to see if the door remains flat—it may be necessary to recramp the door and tap the wedges further in if it remains curved. When the door is flat, cramp it up again, mark the wedges for length, remove them and cut them to the correct size. Glue them up and replace them, allowing the adhesive to dry before removing the cramps for the last time.

You can then plane the wedges flush, fill the saw cuts with wood putty and repaint the door. If possible, change the hanging side of the door so that the hinges keep the repaired stile true (see pages 705 to 709).

Altering the doorstop
The easiest solution to the problem of a twisted door is to alter the doorstop, though this sometimes has the dis-advantage of being unsightly. Planted

doorstops are removed simply by prising them away from the frame with a bolster or screwdriver. But first run the point of a knife down the inner corners of the stop on both sides to prevent unnecessary damage being done to the paintwork.

Remove only those stops on the lock side and along the top of the door; leave the stop on the hinging side where it is. Push the door to its closing position, filing the lock's striking plate if necessary. Remove the old nails from the stop, then re-nail the stops so that they bed as consistently as possible against the door. Fill the old nail holes before repainting the stops.

In bad cases, the stop will form an unsightly margin with the architrave and you may have to plane it slightly to follow the contour.

If the doorstop is rebated, you will have to cut the stop to the new alignment. Remove the striking plate, close the door until it touches the stop, then measure the gap at its widest point. Plane a small block of wood to this size to use as a gauge. Place the block against the edge of the door where it touches the stop and, with a pencil on one side of the block, run it up the length of the door mark-ing a line on the doorstop. This will show how much wood you have to remove to accommodate the warp.

Score down the line with a metal straightedge and a sharp knife to prevent the paint from tearing back. Repeat the operation on the inside edges of the stop. Then, starting at the narrowest end, cut in towards the lining with a firmer chisel and a mallet. Alternate your downward cuts with cuts into the inner corner of the

stop, but do not cut below the level of the lining. When all the wood is removed, use a rebate plane to tidy up the inside edges. Finally, replace the striking plate in a different location and chisel out a new rebate to engage with the lock on the door.

Frame repairs
The most common form of damage to door frames is wet rot, which may make the timber swell and con-sequently cause the door to stick or parts of the frame to pull away from their wall mountings.

Depending on the extent of the damage, you may be able to remove the rotted section and patch it with new timber. If so, you should use a lapped joint and secure the new section to the wall with masonry bolts as described on pages 1453 to

9 *Run the point of a sharp knife down the joint between frame and stop to prevent the paint on the frame tearing as you remove the stop*

10 *Using a piece of scrap timber to protect the paintwork on the frame, carefully lever the stop away from the frame with a screwdriver*

11 *Carefully plane the stop down to the line you have drawn, and then repeat the procedure for the stop along the top of the door*

13 *Before modifying a warped door, take it off its hinges, lay it flat, then remove the lock and handle plus any beading around the panels*

14 *Use a straightedge to find out how badly the door stile is warped, and to discover where the warp is most pronounced*

15 *Use a sliding bevel to mark out a symmetrical wedge on the stile where the warp is greatest—here it is next to the lock*

Simon Butcher

16 *Use the bevel again to mark out 'dovetails' on the edge of the stile. Symmetry is very important as the wedge must fit properly*

17 *Mark the depth of the cut-out with a marking gauge, ensuring that this is the same as the depth of the panels in the door*

18 *You can now make a series of vertical cuts in the wedge with a tenon saw. Be careful not to damage the panel as you do so*

Repairs and renovations

1457. For a professional finish, lay a strip of polyethylene or PVC between the repair and the masonry, and re-seal all the joints at the wall with a non-hardening mastic. This prevents the wet from attacking timber from behind, where it is unprotected by the paint on its outer faces.

Bear in mind that although paint protects the timber beneath it, urban grime attacks the paint and gradually reduces its effectiveness to the point where rot can gain a foothold. Regular cleaning therefore helps to protect the timber from rot and also enables you to identify problem areas before it is too late. You will quite probably see the first signs of rot as bubbling on the paint's surface.

If the rot is too extensive to be patched, you will have to instal a new frame. Fortunately, this is a less daunting prospect than it seems. Your first step is to measure the dimensions of your opening and the size of your

D. *One method of curing warps in a panelled door. The saw cuts should go no deeper than the level of the panels, and the wedges should stick out at both ends when hammered in*

door—assuming that you do not wish to alter the dimensions—and to either purchase a frame of the appropriate size and dimensions, or to make one yourself (a technique covered further on in the Carpentry course).

Many larger timber or builders' merchants supply door sets consisting of a door and door frame with all surfaces sealed and primed, a lock, lift-off hinges, and full fitting instructions. These save time and a good deal of work. But if you need only to replace the frame, measure up the old one—particularly its overall width and height—and purchase a new one compatible with your existing door.

If you want to refit the old door, the inside jamb measurement will need to be the width of the door or less; it will be no good if the door is too small for the frame, though you can plane down a door that is too big.

Remove the door and place it on its side out of the way. If the door frame is butted against the floor and not built into a wooden threshold (see pages 713 to 716), prise it loose carefully with a crow-bar working from the bottom upwards. If the horns of the top rail are built into the wall,

use an old saw to cut through the rail then prise it off, wriggling both ends free from their mountings. Where the frame has a built-in hardwood threshold, do the same here so that you can prise the jambs free from the wall.

When the frame is out, brush down the walls and examine them. Sometimes frames are fitted to brick walls by screwing to wooden blocks built in to the brickwork and if this is the case you may be able to use the existing blocks. But remove them if they are loose or rotten and insert new ones, making sure that they are firmly packed and mortared into the brickwork. With a heavy pencil or chalk, mark the positions of the blocks on the wall to one side of where the frame will stand. This will make it easier to locate and screw into them.

Next, put the frame in position and use a level or plumbline to establish the vertical. Lightly mark the frame opposite the blocks in the wall as a guide for drilling the screw holes. Then remove it and drill countersunk holes which you can fill later.

Place the frame back in position, level it and check its diagonal dimensions to make sure that it is true;

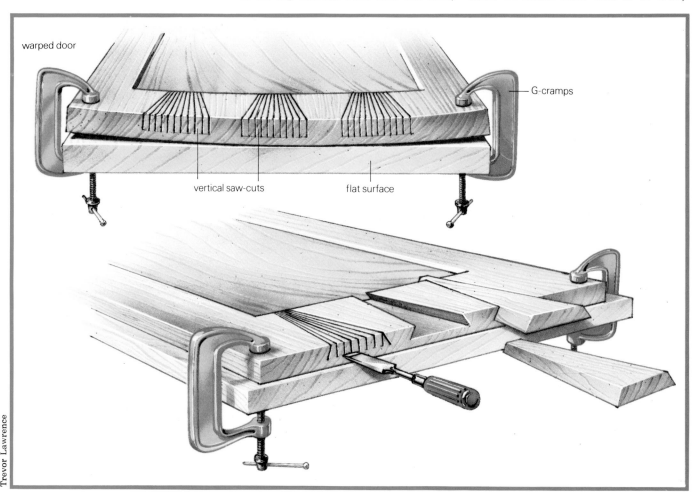

warped door

G-cramps

vertical saw-cuts

flat surface

19 *When you have made the saw cuts, remove the waste with a bevel edged chisel. Try to get the cut-out as flat and smooth as possible*

20 *If you did not angle the two outermost saw cuts, use a chisel to undercut them and so provide a firm grip for the wedge*

21 *Mark the outline of the wedge on a piece of softwood using the sliding bevel. Make sure you do so across the grain of the wood*

22 *Tap the wedge firmly into place with a mallet until it overcomes the warp and causes the door to lie flat along the workbench*

23 *Once the door is flat you can mark the cutting lines on the wedge to indicate the waste wood that must be removed*

24 *Then gently tap out the wedge and apply a liberal coating of PVA woodworking or urea formaldehyde adhesive to all the contact surfaces*

Simon Butcher

then fix it to the wooden blocks using No. 8 woodscrews 75–100mm long. You may need to pack small battens between the frame and the wall to take up any unevenness, so bear this in mind and keep checking the squareness of the frame as you screw into the bricks or studs.

If the old frame is fixed with galvanized steel cramps, you will be unable to re-use the old cramps. So, when you place the frame in its experimental position, mark on it suitable positions for fixing screws drilled directly into the masonry. You will have to drill into firm brickwork—not the mortar joints—so mark the positions accordingly. Then remove the frame and drill at least three holes on each jamb to take No. 8 or 10 countersunk wood-screws 65–100mm long. Afterwards, replace the frame,

level it, and check its diagonal dimensions to ensure it is square.

Wedge the frame temporarily in its true position, and mark through the drill holes into the brickwork with a long masonry nail. Then, before you remove the frame, mark its position clearly on the wall so that you can match the holes later.

With this done, remove it and drill the holes in the brickwork with a masonry bit of the correct size. Insert wall plugs to match the screw size you are using and replace the frame aligned with the marks just made.

Finally, to finish off the project, fill all the holes in the frame with a proprietary wood filler and then point around the door frame with a 1:3 mortar mix. When the mortar has set apply a liberal amount of non-hardening mastic to all the joints.

25 *To prevent damage to the door, cut off the thin end of the wedge before you replace it. Then trim off the waste on the thick end*

Building brickwork arches

● Types of brick arch ● Designing an arch ● Choosing the correct bricks ● Erecting and reinforcing a soldier arch ● Ringed arch construction: building plans, erecting a former and bricklaying ● Pointing and finishing off

Below: *Arches are relatively easy to build for anyone who has mastered basic bricklaying. Even rounded arches like the ringed arch can be tackled since this involves no complicated geometry or cutting of bricks to form the shape*

Simon Butcher

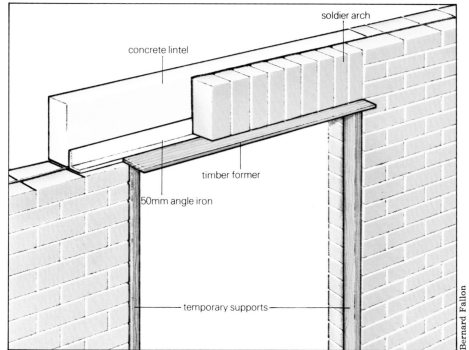

soldier arch

concrete lintel

timber former

50mm angle iron

temporary supports

Bernard Fallon

A. Above: *To construct a soldier arch above an opening you need a concrete lintel to take the weight from above as well as a piece of angle iron to support the brickwork*

Decorative brickwork arches over doorways, windows and small alcoves can turn an otherwise dull opening into an elegant and distinctive feature. And building a brick arch is not as difficult as it might appear. The key to success lies in already having some knowledge of basic bricklaying (see pages 20 to 25 and 132 to 137) and in careful preparation before you start any building work.

Varieties of brick arch
A large number of brick arches—such as the gothic, segmental or axed arch—are extremely difficult to erect and need years of experience to execute successfully. But there are two basic types—the *soldier* arch and the *ringed* arch—which anyone with basic bricklaying skills can build.
Soldier arch: This is a square-shaped arch which is purely decorative and non-loadbearing. Generally it is used to cover the reinforced lintel or rolled steel joist that bears the weight of the wall from above and which is placed behind it (fig. A).

The exact design of the arch varies according to the position of the lintel and the thickness of the wall into which it is built. A single leaf wall or an opening backing on to an existing house wall usually has a brick arch on only one side of the opening, while a double thick or cavity wall has an arch on both sides.
Ringed arch: This is the simplest type of rounded arch to construct since it involves no complex geometry or cutting of bricks to fit the design. It is semi-circular in shape with all of the bricks facing inwards towards the centre of the arch. To add a decorative finish, two or even three rows of brick are often set on end—one above the other.

Once you decide the type of arch you want to build, familiarize yourself with some of the terms used in arch construction. Fig. D shows all the component parts of a typical ringed brickwork arch.

Arch design
Brickwork arches can be built as part of a new wall construction or inserted into an existing wall over a door, window, or other suitable opening.

If you are building a new wall and want to include brick arches as part of the overall construction, site them carefully and make sure they are included on building plans. Design door and window openings so they are just wide enough to build an arch using a convenient number of whole bricks. Also, take into account how any proposed arch will look once it is built—avoid over-large arches which look out of place above a small opening, such as a narrow door.

Once your plans are drawn up and the site prepared, start work on building the wall. Continue until you reach a level where the arch can be inserted easily and conveniently. If you are building a ringed arch, stop when the top of the last course is level with the springing line (fig. D); for a soldier arch, build up to a level one course below the arch itself.

If you are inserting a new arch into an existing wall, you must first of all demolish the brickwork above the opening. Try to cut away the minimum number of bricks in case you start a general collapse. Treat openings wider than 1m with great care and carry out tests to determine whether the wall is loadbearing before any demolition takes place (see pages 988 to 991).

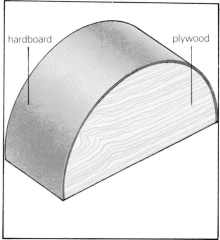

hardboard   plywood

B. Above: *A ringed arch is easily constructed if you build a timber former. This supports the brickwork above the opening while the arch is being built*

Before you actually cut away any brickwork, decide the size and shape of arch you want and mark its outline in chalk across the top of the opening. Then, starting from the bottom, use a hammer and wide bolster to chop out one brick at a time and carefully remove it (see pages 222 to 227). Wear goggles or safety glasses when doing this to protect your eyes.

Once you have removed all the bricks within the marked-out area, chop out a further amount—equal to about one course—all around the opening. This will allow you enough room to work when erecting the new arch. Clear away all the debris left around the opening at this stage and lightly dampen the surrounding brickwork with water and a distemper brush to cut down the dust.

1 To build a ringed arch above an existing opening, first measure the distance across the opening and then calculate its midpoint

2 From this point, extend a line upwards and draw a large semi-circle across the brickwork to mark the underside of the arch

3 Measure and extend this circle by a further amount so that you can cut away enough bricks to build the arch without being cramped

Simon Butcher

7 Extend a piece of string from the mid-point of the line and tie a pencil to its top end. Use this to mark the two former sides

8 Cut carefully around the marked-out line. You can use a fretsaw, although a powered jig saw makes the job a great deal easier

9 Cut a piece of timber to make up the bottom of the former and nail the two side pieces to it using galvanized nails

Selecting bricks

Before starting work on the arch, it is important to make sure that the bricks you are going to use are exactly the right type and colour. If your arch is part of a new construction, you should have few problems getting bricks which match those on the wall behind. But if you are inserting a new arch into an existing wall, you may well have difficulty getting bricks which are similar—especially if the existing bricks are old.

To solve this problem, take one of the bricks from the wall to a builders' merchants or brickyard. They should be able to provide you with a selection of secondhand bricks, some of which will hopefully match those in the wall. If you have no success, search out a demolition contractor's yard for an alternative source.

To add an extra decorative dimension, the arch can be built with bricks of a different colour to those on the existing wall.

Erecting a soldier arch

As a soldier arch is purely decorative rather than loadbearing, first position a concrete lintel or rolled steel joist across the middle or back of the opening. If the span of the opening is less than 1.8m, you can easily reinforce the lintel on site by the addition of steel rods in the mortar mix (see pages 1464 to 1469).

Once the lintel is in place, position a piece of 50mm angle iron in front of it. Make sure that this is long enough to bear on the brickwork on each side of the opening by at least 150mm and that the angle faces inwards away from the lintel to support one edge of the brickwork across the arch (see pages 1464 to 1469).

The angle iron alone will not bear the whole weight of the arch during construction, so the next step is to build a simple timber former and place it across the top of the opening directly below the arch (fig. A). Get a piece of 25mm thick timber the same width as the *soffit*—the underside of the proposed arch—and cut it to the exact length of the opening.

To hold the former in position, cut two 15mm square supports the same width as the soffit from offcuts of batten and secure them with concrete nails on each side of the opening (fig. A). Then place the former on top of the supports, check it carefully with a spirit level, and adjust as necessary before continuing.

Now you can start work on the arch

4 Use a hammer and bolster to cut away the brickwork. Some openings have a piece of reinforced steel which needs to be removed

5 Continue upwards carefully, removing one brick at a time, until a large enough area has been cleared to start building

6 Make the sides of the former from 15mm plywood. First draw a line the same size as the opening across the bottom of the sheet

10 Then pin a piece of hardboard on thin plywood across the top of the former. Try to keep it level with the two side pieces

11 To support the former, fix a length of 50mm square timber to each side of the soffit using masonry nails or wall plugs and screws

12 Then lay a piece of flat plywood almost as wide as the soffit across the tops of the side bearers to complete the frame

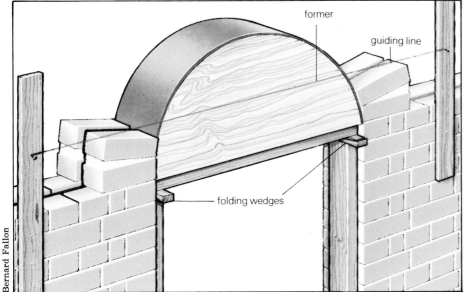

former

guiding line

folding wedges

Bernard Fallon

itself. First measure across the opening and note the proposed position of the bricks (do this on both sides of the wall if you are erecting two arches). Using this information, try to place the *key*—or middle-brick—directly over the centre of the opening and so avoid having to place a shorter, cut brick at one end of the arch.

Mortar each brick into place carefully and place a straightedge across the face of the wall while you are building to ensure that the arch is correctly aligned. When you have finished, leave the mortar to set for three to four days. Then carefully

C. Left: *When building a ringed arch, the former is supported on a temporary frame across the opening. Strings stretched across the arch help to keep bricks in line*

13 To help you adjust the position of the former, cut four folding wedges and position them in pairs underneath each end

14 Then check that the former is correctly positioned and in line with the existing wall using a straightedge and spirit level

15 Start at the bottom of the arch, building each side at the same pace. The bricks can be set either on edge or on end, according to plan

16 Try to make neat, wedge-shaped joints between each brick by laying more mortar at one end than at the other before positioning them

17 A line stretched up from the striking point ensures that each brick is correctly placed and facing inwards towards the centre

18 You can rebuild the brickwork around the arch as you progress or leave this until the whole arch has been completed

19 Point the brickwork on and around the arch carefully. Then rake a soft brush across the whole area to help it to blend in

20 Leave the mortar to set for around three to four days before carefully knocking out the wedges and removing the former

remove the former and knock away its supporting timbers.

Finally, point the brickwork across the face and soffit of the arch. If you are fitting a new arch into older brickwork, try to point some way around it so that the new mortar is less obvious.

Building a ringed arch

Making a success of a ringed arch depends on careful preparation and planning before the actual building takes place. This involves drawing a plan of the arch on paper and then using this both to calculate the amount of materials you need and to plan construction of a timber former. Once the former is built, you place it under the arch to support the bricks during building.

Former plan: Start by drawing a

Simon Butcher

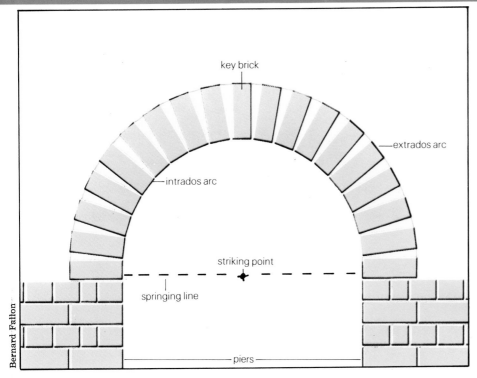

key brick

extrados arc

intrados arc

striking point

springing line

piers

Bernard Fallon

D. Above: *A sound knowledge of the component parts of a ringed arch is essential if you want to build one correctly. Note that all the bricks face towards the striking point*

life-size plan of the intrados arc (fig. D) on a large piece of paper or card. Measure across the springing line at the top of the opening, then go to the paper and draw a line of the same dimension across the bottom of the sheet. Mark the midpoint of the line carefully and this will give you the striking point of the arch.

With this, the base line of the arch, marked, use the striking point as a centre and draw a semi-circle above the springing line with a large compass or a pencil tied to the end of a piece of string. Then lay a square or protractor along the springing line and draw a line up from the striking point which bisects the half-circle (fig. D). This gives the exact position of the key brick.

Use the half circle and the perpendicular line running up through it to mark the position of each brick on the plan. Make sure all the bricks face inwards towards the striking point and that they are separated by neat, wedge-shaped joints.

Once the plan is drawn out—using one or more rows of brick—it can be used to calculate the exact number of bricks needed to complete the job. Remember, though, that the total has to be doubled in a cavity or double

thickness wall where the arch has to be reproduced on both sides of a door or window opening.

Former construction: To construct the former, you need a sheet of 15mm plywood to make up the rounded sides and the soffit plus a piece of hardboard to go across the top.

Mark the two semicircular side pieces first, to the same dimensions as the plan. Cut them out carefully using a fretsaw. Then cut a third piece as wide as the soffit—excluding the two side sections—and as long as the opening. Attach the three pieces together by nailing along the bottom of the two side sections into the edge of the soffit section (figs 6 to 9).

With the frame completed, pin a piece of hardboard as wide as the soffit across the top and make sure that it is flat and level with the two sides (fig. 10). After you have re-checked the former against the original plan, locate it in position across the top of the opening.

Supporting the former: To hold the timber former in place during construction, you must build a small frame to fit underneath. This should consist of two side pieces with one wider cross-piece which fits across the top—although in the case of particularly wide soffits two frames may have to be built, one for each side.

First measure the distance from the ground to the springing line. Subtract the width of the cross support, then cut two side bearers from 50mm

square timber to this size. Fix the side bearers to the brickwork in the middle of the soffit using masonry or galvanized nails (fig. 11).

Next, lay a piece of flat plywood almost as wide as the soffit across the top of the side bearers. Check carefully that it is correctly aligned with a spirit level and then place the timber former on top (fig. 12).

Finally, cut four folding timber wedges and drive two from each side between the cross-piece and the side bearers. These allow you to make minor adjustments to the position of the former during construction and make it easier to remove it after the mortar has set (fig. 13).

Building the arch: To help keep the arch brickwork level with the face of the wall, nail four flat boards about 500mm long on each side of the opening extending from the top to the bottom of the arch. Then attach a string across the bottom of each pair of boards to act as a guiding line—this can be moved up as building progresses (fig. C).

Start at the bottom of the arch, building each side at the same pace. As you position each brick check—with the help of a line stretched up from the striking point—that it is correctly positioned according to the original plan (fig. 17).

Try to make neat, wedge-shaped mortar joints between each brick by putting more mortar on one end than you do at the other (fig. 16). Alternatively, insert small wedging pieces of slate between each brick and leave them permanently to set with the mortar.

Continue upwards until you reach the key brick, raising the guiding lines as you go. Check carefully that the final bricks are positioned correctly, especially the key brick which sits directly above the middle of the opening (fig. D).

Leave the mortar to set for at least three to four days—then knock away the folding wedges and remove the former (fig. 20). Finally, pull the side supports away from the wall and point the brickwork on the arch.

Take great care when you are building or rebuilding the brickwork around the top of the arch, and use the lines you erected earlier as guides. Try to ensure that each brickwork course meets the sides of the arch neatly, and cut any bricks to fit with a hammer and bolster. Point around the outside of the entire area and then—while the mortar is still wet—run a soft brush across the surface.

Making the most of alcoves

Many people are lost for ideas when confronted with an alcove, but alcoves are definitely a furnishing asset—whether used to house bookshelves or a dining table and chairs—and it is up to you to exploit them to best advantage

Spike Powell

Alcoves lend themselves particularly well to providing built-in storage space and this can be made with the minimum of skill, time and expense. Shelving is particularly easy to fit since shelf supports are fixed to the two opposing walls of the alcove.

For a really neat finish, tailor your shelving to the exact depth of the alcove. Shelving can be made of solid wood and supported by battens at either end of the alcove—and with an extra batten running along the back if the shelves cover a wide span.

Veneered chipboard provides less expensive shelving, but if the shelves are to take heavy weights, such as books, an extra supporting batten is definitely needed and one along the front is a good idea.

Shelves can also be made of plywood, or even of hardboard if supported on a timber frame. If you want your shelves to be adjustable, support them with brackets fitted to two slotted wall channels running up the back wall of the alcove or use slotted metal strips with slot-in clips running up each of the side walls.

Shelving ideas

Shelved alcoves can be made more sophisticated by including a simple cupboard built into the bottom half. This entails little work, since the walls of the alcove form the back and sides of the cupboard and all that is needed to complete the effect is to fit doors to the front frame.

Ready-made doors are available in panelled and louvre styles, and the overall arrangement can be planned to give an attractive built-in 'dresser' effect which could be enhanced with a moulded pelmet across the top, and with mouldings added to the shelf edge. Use the top of the cupboard as a display shelf.

Shelved alcoves can also provide useful storage in rooms all around the house. In living rooms, use alcoves for books, varying the space between shelves to accommodate the different sizes of your book collections.

Elizabeth Whiting

Above: *An antique bed recessed into a deep bedroom alcove creates the effect of a room within a room. Careful measurement of both furniture and alcove is vital when considering such arrangements*

Alternatively use the alcove to provide built-in spaces for your television or hi-fi, or build a cocktail cabinet with spaces for bottles, decanters, glasses and accessories.

By adding simple containers to alcove shelves you can provide convenient storage space for sewing kit, toys, cards and games and other forms of household clutter.

In the hall, an alcove fitted with hooks for coats and a rack at the bottom for shoes makes a handy storage area. A hall alcove could also be kitted out as a place to keep cleaning materials, with spring hooks or a slotted rack to keep brooms, bins for polishes, cloths and other materials.

Bedroom alcoves can be turned into dressing tables simply by adding a shelf and a mirror. If the alcove is needed for storage, it can be lined with shelves and plastic pull-out bins—such as washing-up bowls or shoe boxes—as a cheap way of providing drawer space. Such an arrangement could be concealed with a pull-down roller blind or a curtain.

For wardrobe space, special pull-out rod hanging fitments are available for hanging clothes, or a shelf can be fitted with a hanging rod running underneath. A blind or curtain could again be used for concealment.

A more ambitious storage arrangement would be to turn the alcove into a fitted cupboard, using its sides and back as the sides and back of the cupboard and simply fitting doors and a frame at the front.

However, most alcoves are too shallow to provide the 525mm depth needed to satisfactorily hang clothes, and the built-in cupboard will therefore need to project slightly into the room. With such an arrangement, narrow shelving could be run around the rest of the room to provide a neat, flush appearance.

Bathroom and kitchen

In the bathroom an alcove could be fitted with shelving to take towels, bottles and other bathroom clutter. Here, even a very shallow alcove with shelves as little as 100mm deep is still very handy for storing mugs, soap dishes, shaving kit, talcum powders and other toiletries.

In the kitchen, an alcove with shelving and perhaps a built-in cupboard can be very useful; but the alcove could also be used to partly recess bulky equipment into the wall.

Michael Boys

Above: *Small alcoves provide ideal settings for house plants but here, the alcove is also used to store logs for firewood. The combined effect makes the most of the carefully restored brickwork*

If a kitchen has been added on to your house, you may be left with an alcove where the windows of the old external wall were. A fridge or, if it is convenient to plumb in, a washing machine could be recessed there.

If kitchen alcoves are not deep enough to provide major storage areas, they can still be lined with shallow shelving to take mugs, glasses, spice jars, jams and conserves, and other kitchen equipment.

An alcove anywhere in the home can be fitted with a seat to make a comfortable spot for reading, lounging or answering the telephone. Build a simple box fitment into the alcove and add a foam cushion covered with an attractive fabric. A lift-up lid could be added to provide additional storage space. This seating/storage arrangement looks particularly attractive underneath a window.

When fitted with a deep shelf and a chair, an alcove makes a simple, but serviceable working desk. Shallower shelves can be added higher up to store books, files and papers.

Decorative effects

It is worth taking extra trouble when you have an alcove with a window. Many people simply curtain off the whole area by running a rail or rod across the front of the alcove, thus cutting it off from the rest of the room at night. This is a waste of both space and decorative potential. Curtain tracks are available which can be bent by hand around the insides of the alcove so that the curtains can be pulled back around the walls by day. Alternatively, you could fit a simple roller blind which would not cut the alcove off from the rest of the room when pulled down at night.

Alcoves are especially good for creating decorative effects a little out of the ordinary. You could decorate the alcove in a different wallcovering from the rest of the room—perhaps using something special such as paper-backed silk, grasscloth or metallic paper. This could then be used as a backdrop for shelving and to enhance any decorative objects on display. A less expensive—but equally effective—method is to paint the alcove walls a tone or two deeper than the colour chosen for the rest of the room.

Mirrors, too, can be used to enhance an alcove, and they will give a feeling of extra space in the rest of the room. You can buy the mirror in a large piece and fix it to the wall with mirror-screws with domed chrome heads; or you could cover the wall with mirror tiles, fixed with self-

Above: *An unusual alcove deserves special treatment. This one makes the best use of window light to display house plants*

Michael Boys

adhesive pads. Bronzed mirrors are more sophisticated, and perhaps less disturbing for people in the room as their reflections are dimmed.

In all these arrangements, whether with shelves or mirrors, a grander, 'period' effect can be created by building arches over the tops of the alcoves—adding plaster mouldings if desired.

Where two alcoves flank a chimney breast, remember that there is no need for each to be treated in the same

way. In fact it often looks better if the shelf arrangements do not exactly match, although they should balance each other. If the fireplace has been removed, it is possible to treat one alcove and the chimney breast as a unit, leaving the other alcove mostly empty. You can build deep shelves projecting from one alcove and continue shallower shelves across the face of the chimney breast, with perhaps one deep shelf at seating height across the remaining alcove.

Now that you have taken the trouble to give your alcoves a special decorative treatment, make sure that the possessions you put on display do your ideas justice. An alcove is the perfect place to show off a treasured collection of old glass, silver, or a particular colour or make of china, or carved ivory animals, painted eggs or wooden boxes. Consider using glass or mirrored shelves for added glamour. Or use an alcove for a stunning display of leafy plants, or vases of fresh or dried flowers,

When setting up alcove displays, pay particular attention to lighting. Slim, fluorescent strips can be used to provide lighting at the front or back of

alcove shelving and the lamp can be concealed with a narrow strip of wood. If a gap is left between the back of the shelves and the walls, lighting can be used very effectively to flood the back of the wall. You can also light an alcove from the front, using a spotlight trained on the objects you wish to highlight.

Finally, a word of warning. If you do not want to fill in an alcove with built-in storage spaces or shelving, but prefer to use it to set off an interesting piece of furniture, be sure to take the alcove measurements with you when you go hunting around furniture or junk shops.

Remember that alcoves on either

side of a fireplace are not necessarily exactly the same size, particularly in old houses. Measure the alcove at the skirting board, and again further up the wall. And, when shopping, beware of furniture which may have a projecting piece around the top which might prevent it from fitting into an alcove: always measure furniture at its widest point.

Below: *Kitchen alcoves are especially useful as storage space. Note the use of the fireplace as a second alcove*

Left inset: *A prized piece of furniture both displayed and protected by recessing it in a living room alcove*

Making a staircase

● **Designing a straight run staircase** ● **The important design considerations** ● **Traditional and simplified designs** ● **Setting out your design** ● **Transferring the design to timber** ● **How to assemble the staircase**

Ray Duns

Left: *Building a timber staircase requires no special carpentry skills or tools, although the integrity of the construction demands care. The most difficult part of such a project is getting your design to comply with local building regulations*

Flight rise: The vertical distance, measured against a plumb, between two floors or a floor and a landing.

Open riser: A stairway having no risers, sometimes called open plan or ladder stairs

Common stairway: A stairway, either inside or outside a building, intended for use by the occupants of more than one dwelling

Construction

Stairs can be constructed between walls, which give a continuous support, or they may be open on one or both sides.

The treads are supported in all cases by stringers. Wall stringers can be 32mm planed all round timber, but outer stringers should be 44mm to 50mm planed all round timber because of the greater strain they bear.

Where a stair width exceeds 900mm you must make an intermediate support or *carriage* from 100mm×50mm timber. This should be fixed at the top and the bottom of the staircase either by nailing it to a joist or by making a birdsmouth cut over the battens nailed across the floor and the landing trimmer of the higher level.

It is usual to fill in the underside of the staircase with a plasterboard soffit. But if you wish to do this you must either extend the width of the stringers to allow the plasterboard an area of purchase or screw 25mm bearers to the insides of the stringers so that you extend their depth.

The width of the timber for the stringers depends both on the angle or *pitch* of the stairs and on the size of the treads and risers. Allowing for a 38mm–40mm margin, 225mm wide boards are normally sufficient. But if you do need to use wider boards, which are not available in softwood, you should join two boards with moulded tongued-and-grooved joints.

In the case of a wall stringer attached to a wall which is to be plastered later, you must rebate the upper outside edge of the board to take the plaster and mould the inside

The most economical way to connect two different levels is with a staircase. And there is no reason why, armed with basic carpentry skills, you should not design and build your own staircase. This part of the course deals with the construction of a staircase run—turning a corner is dealt with further on in the course.

The design of staircases, like many other major projects, is controlled by statutory regulations concerning strength, stability, fire resistance and general safety factors.

So that you can understand the regulations and any construction drawings you may need to use, make sure you are familiar with the following terms used in staircase design and

also the names of the component parts shown in figs A, B and C.

Pitch line: A line joining the front edges of the treads (nosings)

Pitch or slope: The angle between the pitch line and the floor or landing

Headroom: The vertical distance between the nosings and any overhead obstruction

Walking line: The average position taken up by a person climbing or descending the stairs, usually taken to be 450mm from the hand rail

Going: The on-plan measurement of a tread between the nosing of that tread and the nosing of the tread or landing above

Rise: The vertical distance between the upper surfaces of two treads

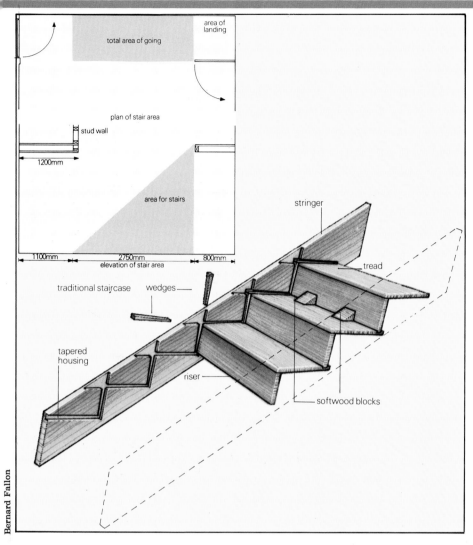

area of landing

total area of going

plan of stair area

stud wall

1200mm

area for stairs

1100mm   2750mm   800mm
elevation of stair area

traditional staircase   wedges

tapered housing

stringer

tread

riser

softwood blocks

A. Above: *To assemble the traditional design of staircase, softwood wedges are inserted into the tapered housing spaces beneath the treads and risers then triangular blocks are glued and pinned into place.* **Inset**: *The first stage is to make a plan of, and section through, the proposed staircase*

edge to match any skirtings. To match perfectly, the stringer must project beyond the plaster by the same amount as the skirtings. This requires no small measure of skill, but you can simplify the project by building the staircase of a different, contrasting material to the skirtings. The polished wood of the former will then complement the painted finish of the latter.

The treads are usually made from 32mm planed all round timber and the risers from either 25mm timber or 12.5mm plywood. You can use softwood or hardwood, but if the steps are to be left uncarpeted the latter is the natural choice. Open tread stairs have no risers to support the treads,

therefore the boards must be at least 38mm thick.

If your project is along traditional lines, you may well be able to find pre-shaped and grooved boards for the stair treads at your timber yard.

The nosings must never exceed 25mm to avoid catching toes when mounting the stairs. There are three shapes of nosing in common use—square, half round, and tapered.

The housings in the stringers for the treads and risers are usually between 9mm and 16mm deep, though the average depth is 13mm. Traditionally they are made wider than the tread and riser boards, and are tapered so that they can be wedged (fig. A).

The wedges are first dipped in adhesive and inserted from the back of the risers and treads. They are then driven home, so forcing each tread and riser against the outer, visible edge of the housing. Finally, triangular blocks of wood are glued and pinned at the junctions of the treads, risers and stringers to make the assembly rigid.

Open riser stairs cannot be wedged and blocked, so alternative methods of construction must be employed. Normally, the treads are housed in the stringer and held in position with screws or dowels. Dowels are stronger than screws, but if you do not want to see the dowel end grain you should use thin screws and plugging pellets (fig. 11). If you opt for the screws, you must pre-drill the end grain of the treads to accept glued fibre wall plugs.

You can strengthen an open riser staircase by tying the stringers together using 10mm or 13mm steel rods—with sunk and pelleted ends—at the back of every fourth tread. You can also use this technique on a simplified version of the traditional staircase (as shown in figs 1 to 11).

Handrails are set at a minimum of 840mm above the pitch line. On the wall side they can be fixed with brackets, screws and plugs at 915mm–1220mm centres. If you use the bracket type, the rail should be at least 38mm from the wall to ensure an adequate hand hold.

Handrails running parallel to an outside stringer are supported either by newel posts at the top and bottom or by a newel post at bottom and a wall fixing at the top of the stairs. The newel posts are mortised to both the stringers and the handrail and the bottom post is let into the floor where it is screwed or bolted to a joist.

Setting out a staircase

To make a staircase it is first of all necessary to make an accurate drawing of the location using as large a scale as is convenient.

1 *Having marked the face side and edges, clamp the two stringers together and mark the template spacings with dividers and a try square*

2 *Separate the stringers, continue the marks to the nosing line then put the template in position over the marks and draw around it*

3 *Use a 1.5mm twist bit to drill marker holes right through the stringers at the point where the screw holes will be drilled later*

4 *Using the bradawl to position the template accurately over the previously traced housing, repeat the tracing to the end of the stringer*

Gavin Cochrane

5 *To remove the waste wood, you can drill a series of holes inside the housing marks using a depth stop to ensure an even depth*

6 *Use a suitable firmer chisel to take small, vertical bites of the waste wood then clear the rest of the waste from the housing*

7 *Finally use a hand router to cut the housing to an even depth and tidy up the inside faces with some glass paper wrapped around a block*

Start by drawing up a plan view of the area in which the staircase is to be situated. You will then be able to work out how much access you need to the staircase and how much room you need to move around the stairs. Also you will be able to see the total length of going available to you.

Draw a side elevation of the area, taking care to measure the overall rise from the lower floor level to the floor level of the landing above. Show also any overhead obstructions which may affect the clearance and headroom above the stairs.

To calculate the size of the treads and the risers for any staircase, use the following formula:

$$\frac{\textbf{Total going}}{\textbf{Projected number of treads}} = \textbf{Actual going}$$

To find the rise, use the formula:

$$\frac{\textbf{Total rise}}{\textbf{Projected number of risers}} = \textbf{Actual rise}$$

The UK building regulations relevant to the construction of staircases state that one going plus two risers must not be less than 600mm and not more than 620mm. So, by adding the actual going and twice the actual riser height obtained from your calculations, you can check if your design is acceptable.

For example, consider a fairly steep staircase with a restricted overall going of 2750mm and an overall rise of 2388mm. The rise multiplied by the going should ideally be 4500mm. Given that there is always one more riser than tread

because the landing acts as the top riser, this staircase needs about 11 or 12 treads; in other words, 12 or 13 risers.

Following the formula described above:

$\frac{2750}{11}$ (total going) (projected number of treads) =250mm—which is acceptable.

On the other hand:
$\frac{2750}{12}$ = 229.16mm—which is better.

Moving on to the rise:
$\frac{2388}{12}$ (overall rise) (projected number of risers) = 199mm—which is just acceptable.

And:
$\frac{2388}{13}$ = 183.69mm—also acceptable.

But in the case of 11 treads, the one going plus two treads sum is 250 + 199 + 199 = 648, which is unacceptable. In the case of 12 treads, however, the sum is 229.16 + 183.69 + 183.69 = 596.54, which is acceptable.

In the example you could therefore start to draw up a staircase with 12 treads, a going of 229.16mm, and 13 risers of 183.69mm.

Having completed the calculations, fill in the outline of the basic steps, and add the details—such as the stringers and the thickness of the nosings—afterwards. Check the headroom, clearance and pitch on the plan, either by using a protractor or with mathematics.

Although it is possible to work solely from this drawing, it is always advisable to finish by drawing up part of the staircase full size—say three risers and two treads—so that you can show as much detail as possible.

Transferring the design to wood
You must use only well seasoned, straight grained timber. Buy this several weeks before it is needed and lay it up in the room where ultimately it will be situated.

Make up a housing template (fig. 2) of 6.5mm hardboard, cutting it as

B. Below left: *A traditional run of stairs using a wedged construction*
C. Below right: *In the simplified design, metal tie rods recessed into the treads hold the run together*

accurately as possible. Make the dimensions of the 'tread' part of the template 1.5mm less all round than the ends of the tread timbers, and the 'riser' part 1mm less all round than the ends of the riser plywood, to allow for cleaning up and sanding the treads before assembly.

Start by marking the stringers with a face side and edge and use a marking gauge to scribe the nosing lines on them. Then cramp the stringers together, face sides inward and face edges uppermost. Use a pair of dividers, a try square and a marking knife to space out and lightly mark the template spacings along the combined face edges (fig. 1). Then separate the stringers and continue these marks across the face sides to meet the nosing lines.

Simplified design: Use the template as shown in fig. 2 to mark out the positions of the housings, screw holes and rod holes.

Then use a 1.5mm twist bit to drill marker holes right through the stringers at the points where screw holes and counterbores will later be drilled.

The next stage is to remove the waste timber from the tread and riser housings. The quickest way to do this is with a template and a router—covered later in the Power tools course.

The alternative method is to remove as much waste wood as possible by drilling a series of holes inside the housing marks. Then remove the rest of the waste with a suitable firmer

chisel, and finish off to an even depth with a hand router.

Now you must cut all the risers to size. Make sure that the grain runs longways. And note that the bottom riser must be one tread thickness narrower than the rest. Follow by cutting the treads to length.

Mark the positions of the riser housings on the treads with a mortise gauge and if possible use a plough plane or multiplane to cut away the waste wood (fig. 8). Then cut the 10mm grooves for the tie rods in the back of every fourth step (fig. 9). And, if your design demands that one or both of the stringers be mortised into the newel post you must prepare the mortises tenons at this stage. Finally, clean up all the cut surfaces and seal the timber as desired.

Assemble the staircase 'dry' and make any necessary adjustments. Then cramp it up and drill through the guide holes into the treads.

Dismantle the completed unit. Locate every screw and rod hole, and counterbore and drill the shank holes for the screws and rods in the outer faces of the stringers. You must also enlarge the pilot holes in the treads so that they are large enough to take 50mm × No. 12 fibre plugs. Finally coat the plugs with PVA wood adhesive and insert them in the holes. Finish by sanding down and sealing the inside surfaces taking care not to seal contact surfaces.

Traditional design: In the case of a

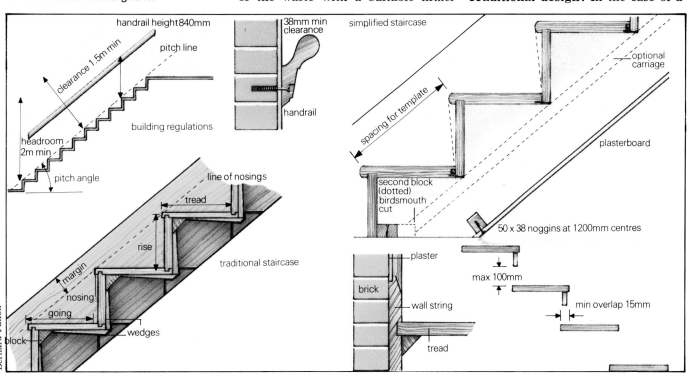

8 *Mark the position of the riser housings on the treads with a mortise gauge and use a plough plane or multiplane to cut out the waste*

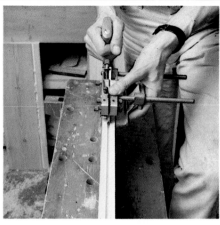

9 *Mark the 10mm groove for the tie rod on the back of the relevant tread and cut it out with a plough plane or a multiplane*

Gavin Cochrane

10 *When screwing into the end-grain, drill a hole and insert a fibre plug smeared with glue in order to stop the timber from splitting*

11 *Once you have assembled the staircase you can insert the tie rods, tighten them, then cover the hole with a suitable wooden plug*

staircase incorporating wooden wedges transferring the design to the wood is identical except for the housings in the stringers. In the simplified design the housings are parallel, but in the traditional design they must be tapered to accept the wedges. Consequently the template must also be given a taper.

Cut tapered housings in the same way as the parallel type, starting them with a powered router and finishing off with a hand router or chisel.

Assembly

You will need eight sash cramps, some timber blocks and a suitable adhesive.

Simplified design: Working on one side at a time, glue and assemble the run in the sideways position, cramp up, then remove the excess adhesive.

Traditional design: In this case lay one of the stringers 'upside down' on the bench and glue into it the top and bottom treads and risers. Apply adhesive to the housings in the other stringer and set this in place with sash cramps. Now make up a number of softwood wedges just thicker than the remaining gaps in top and bottom tread/riser housings. Dip eight of these in adhesive and tap them into the top and bottom sets of housings until the treads and risers are held firm.

You can now slide in and wedge the intervening treads and risers in the same way. As work progresses, the assembly should resemble that shown in fig. A. When the run is complete, glue and pin triangular section blocks at each tread/riser joint. Then re-cramp the entire assembly and leave it to set.

Nail the risers to the treads with 40mm oval nails, punched well below the surface. Then insert the screws and rods, tightening them down as much as possible. Leave the whole unit cramped up for at least 12 hours.

When the adhesive has cured completely you can remove the cramps. Cut plugs or pellets to suit the counterbores, smear them with adhesive and insert them in place. When the adhesive has set, plane the plugs flush with the surrounding surface and finish the outsides of the stringers with sandpaper. The stairway is now ready for installation.

Design considerations
- The rise must not exceed 220mm (190mm on a common stairway) and 140–178mm is thought satisfactory.
- The minimum going is 220mm (230mm minimum for common stairs), but you should try for a 255mm–305mm maximum.
- The maximum pitch is set at 42° to the horizontal and the minimum pitch is 25° (maximum pitch for common stairs is 38°).
- Where any tread has no riser below it, as in open plan or open riser stairs, the nosing of each step must overlap the back of the step below by at least 15mm.
- The gaps between treads on an open riser stairway must be designed in such a way that a solid sphere, 100mm in diameter, will not pass through them.
- The ease with which a stairway may be climbed is dependent upon the proportional relationship between the going and the rise, resulting in the rule that states: for any parallel step, the sum of its going plus twice its rise must equal between 550mm and 620mm.
- There must be no variation in rise or going (parallel steps) for each step in a flight of stairs between consecutive floors.
- Any stairway having a total rise of 600mm or more must have a handrail and adequate guarding extending to 840mm above the pitch line. If the stairway exceeds 1m in width, handrails are required for both sides.
- Ballustrading must be provided to a height of 900mm (1070mm if the staircase is common).
- Infill ballustrading under the handrails should have openings of such dimensions that a solid sphere 100mm diameter, will not pass through them.

Kitchen accessories-1

These functional and attractive pine accessories are cheap and quite simple to make. There are fifteen in all—one to suit every kitchen need. The Project is split into three parts, each featuring five related items

Below: *A selection of co-ordinating pine accessories makes a delightful and practical corner in a kitchen. There are 15 different accessories to mix and match as you wish*
Inset: *The five items featured in Part 1 of the Project*

Fred Mancini

Kitchen accessories are quite expensive to buy, yet these co-ordinated pine fittings are all made from cheap, easy-to-obtain boards. There are 15 items altogether—one for every need—so you can fit out the kitchen as and when you want.

None of them use very complicated techniques. Many of the joints and shapes are common to several items. All the parts can be cut with ordinary hand tools, although an electric router, if you have one, will make the

job of shaping simplicity itself.

The series is divided into three parts, each featuring five accessories. Part 1 covers the fittings shown inset above—four racks for the wall or worktop, and a toast rack.

Similar materials are used throughout. These are mostly 125×19mm softwood for frames, and tongued-and-grooved boards for panelling and as a source of thinner material. You may well be able to obtain offcuts for the small quantities needed.

Follow the working drawings to mark and cut out all the parts. Note that the drawers are common to both the spice rack and the miniature drawer unit. The spice rack can be made in several different versions as shown in the drawings, and you can vary the shelf spacing if you wish to fit a particular size of spice jar.

Finish the edges, then cut out housings and assemble. You must seal all the fittings thoroughly with lacquer, including the backs.

Workplan

Cutting list (large spice rack)
All sizes are in millimetres. Timber is planed all round (PAR) or tongued-and-grooved and V-jointed (T+G+V).

Part	Material	No.	Size
sides	125mm× 19mm softwood (PAR)	2	405mm
horizontals	125mm× 19mm softwood (PAR)	4	450mm× 110mm
drawer dividers	125mm× 19mm softwood (PAR)	2	121mm× 105mm
back panels	100mm× 10mm softwood (T+G+V)	6	430mm
drawer fronts	125mm× 19mm softwood (PAR)	3	128mm× 100mm
drawer backs	100mm× 10mm softwood (T+G+V)	3	128mm× 94mm
drawer sides	100mm× 10mm softwood (T+G+V)	6	94mm× 84mm
drawer bases	6mm plywood	3	128mm× 92mm

Additional material: Panel pins, PVA woodworking adhesive, fixing screws
Finish: Polyurethane or melamine lacquer

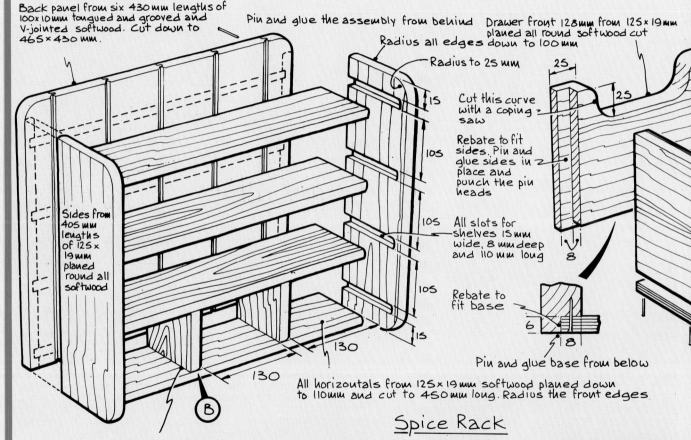

Back panel from six 430mm lengths of 100×10mm tongued and grooved and V-jointed softwood. Cut down to 465×430mm.

Pin and glue the assembly from behind

Drawer front 128mm from 125×19mm planed all round softwood cut down to 100mm

Radius all edges
Radius to 25mm
15
105
105
105
15
Cut this curve with a coping saw
Rebate to fit sides. Pin and glue sides in place and punch the pin heads
All slots for shelves 15mm wide, 8mm deep and 110mm long
Rebate to fit base
Pin and glue base from below
25
25
8
6 8

Sides from 405mm lengths of 125× 19mm planed round all softwood

130
130

All horizontals from 125×19mm softwood planed down to 110mm and cut to 450mm long. Radius the front edges.

Spice Rack

Set in dividers as shown opposite. Dividers are from 125×19mm planed all round softwood cut down to 105mm, and cut 121mm long. Radius the front edges

Alternative designs

Although the working drawings show how to make a large spice rack, you can easily adapt the design to make a smaller rack like the examples shown here. Follow the same basic dimensions and constructions, just leaving out an end or top section

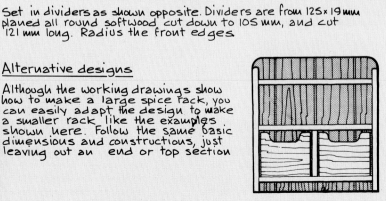
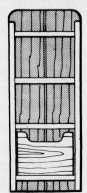

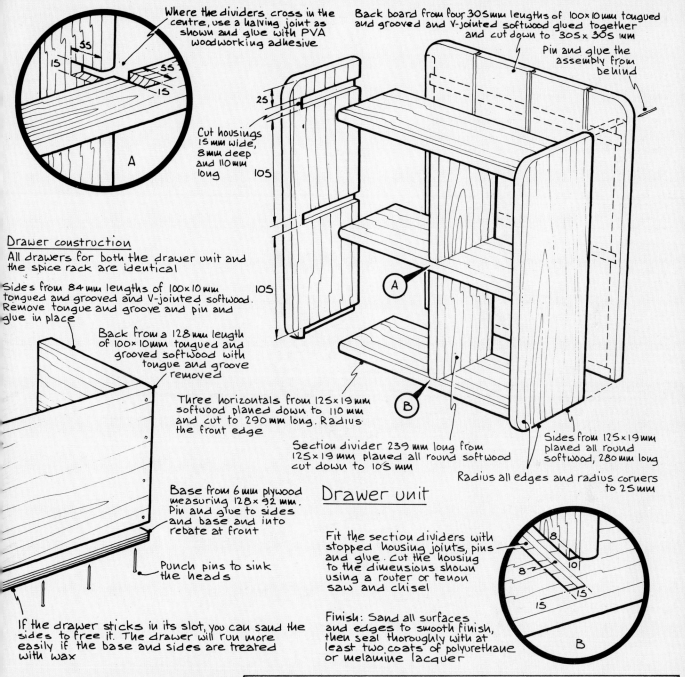

Where the dividers cross in the centre, use a halving joint as shown and glue with PVA woodworking adhesive

Back board from four 305mm lengths of 100×10mm tongued and grooved and V-jointed softwood glued together and cut down to 305×305mm

Pin and glue the assembly from behind

Cut housings 15mm wide, 8mm deep and 110mm long

Drawer construction

All drawers for both the drawer unit and the spice rack are identical

Sides from 84mm lengths of 100×10mm tongued and grooved and V-jointed softwood. Remove tongue and groove and pin and glue in place

Back from a 128mm length of 100×10mm tongued and grooved softwood with tongue and groove removed

Base from 6mm plywood measuring 128×92mm. Pin and glue to sides and base and into rebate at front

Punch pins to sink the heads

If the drawer sticks in its slot, you can sand the sides to free it. The drawer will run more easily if the base and sides are treated with wax

Three horizontals from 125×19mm softwood planed down to 110mm and cut to 290mm long. Radius the front edge

Section divider 239mm long from 125×19mm planed all round softwood cut down to 105mm

Sides from 125×19mm planed all round softwood, 280mm long

Radius all edges and radius corners to 25mm

Drawer unit

Fit the section dividers with stopped housing joints, pins and glue. Cut the housing to the dimensions shown using a router or tenon saw and chisel

Finish: Sand all surfaces and edges to smooth finish, then seal thoroughly with at least two coats of polyurethane or melamine lacquer

Frederick Mancini

Cutting list (miniature drawer unit)

All sizes are in millimetres. Timber is planed all round (PAR) or tongued-and-grooved and V-jointed (T+G+V).

Part	Material	No.	Size
sides	125mm×19mm softwood (PAR)	2	280mm
horizontals	125mm×19mm softwood (PAR)	3	290mm×110mm
drawer divider	125mm×19mm softwood (PAR)	1	239mm×105mm
back panels	100mm×10mm softwood (T+G+V)	4	305mm
drawer fronts	125mm×19mm softwood (PAR)	4	128mm×100mm
drawer backs	100mm×10mm softwood (T+G+V)	4	128mm×94mm
drawer sides	100mm×10mm softwood (T+G+V)	8	94mm×84mm
drawer bases	6mm plywood	4	128mm×92mm

Additional materials: Panel pins, PVA woodworking adhesive, fixing screws
Finish: Polyurethane or melamine lacquer

Project

Fred Mancini

Cutting list (egg rack)

All sizes are in millimetres. Timber is planed all round (PAR) or tongued-and-grooved and V-jointed (T+G+V).

Part	Material	No.	Size
sides	125mm × 19mm softwood (PAR)	2	200mm
back panels	100mm × 10mm softwood (T+G+V)	3	250mm
shelves	100mm × 10mm softwood (T+G+V)	2	206mm

Additional materials: Panel pins, PVA woodworking adhesive, fixing screw

Finish: Polyurethane or melamine lacquer

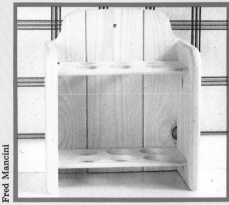

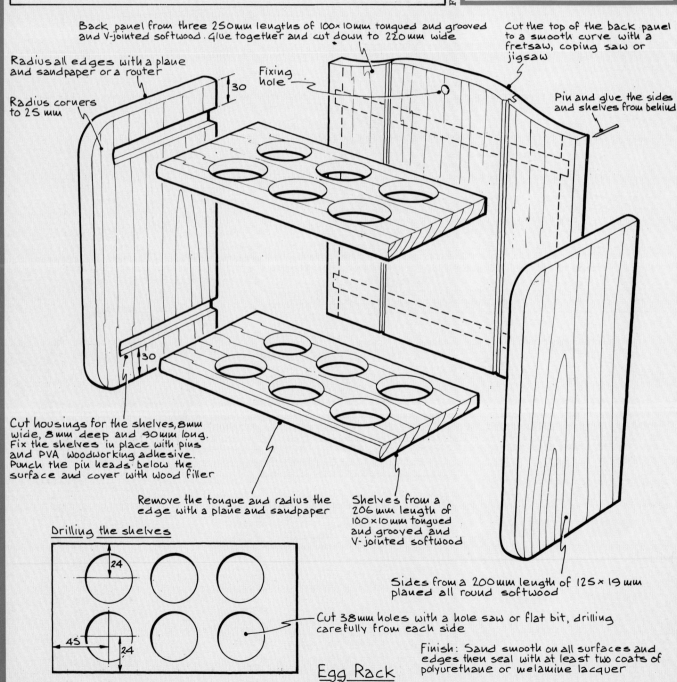

Back panel from three 250mm lengths of 100×10mm tongued and grooved and V-jointed softwood. Glue together and cut down to 220mm wide

Cut the top of the back panel to a smooth curve with a fretsaw, coping saw or jigsaw

Radius all edges with a plane and sandpaper or a router

Fixing hole

Pin and glue the sides and shelves from behind

Radius corners to 25 mm

30

30

Cut housings for the shelves, 8mm wide, 8mm deep and 90mm long. Fix the shelves in place with pins and PVA woodworking adhesive. Punch the pin heads below the surface and cover with wood filler

Remove the tongue and radius the edge with a plane and sandpaper

Shelves from a 206mm length of 100×10mm tongued and grooved and V-jointed softwood

Drilling the shelves

24

45

24

Sides from a 200mm length of 125×19mm planed all round softwood

Cut 38mm holes with a hole saw or flat bit, drilling carefully from each side

Egg Rack

Finish: Sand smooth on all surfaces and edges then seal with at least two coats of polyurethane or melamine lacquer

Cutting list (miniature shelf)
All sizes are in millimetres. Timber is planed all round (PAR) or tongued-and-grooved and V-jointed (T+G+V).

Part	Material	No.	Size
sides	125mm × 19mm softwood (PAR)	2	275mm
shelves	100mm × 10mm softwood (T+G+V)	2	409mm
hook support	100mm × 10mm softwood (T+G+V)	1	393mm × 30mm
back panels	100mm × 10mm softwood (T+G+V)	5	300mm

Additional materials: Panel pins, PVA woodworking adhesive, fixing screws, cuphooks
Finish: Polyurethane or melamine lacquer

Fred Mancini

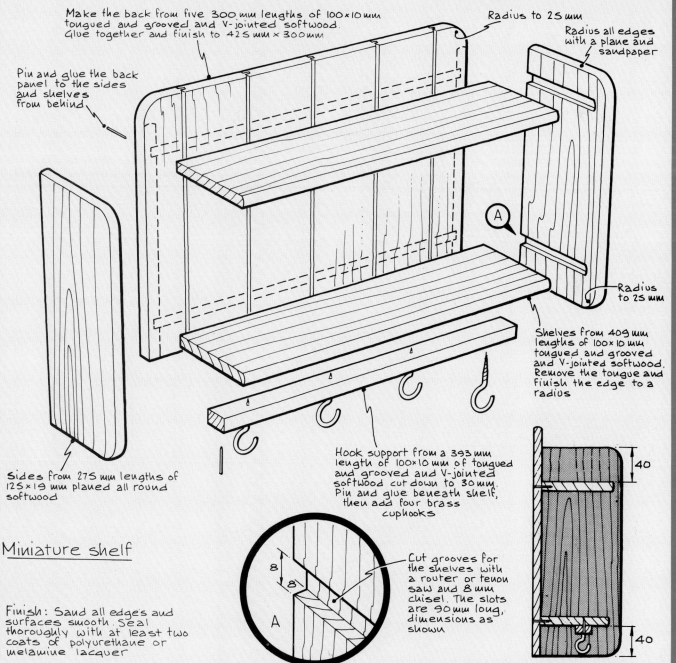

Make the back from five 300 mm lengths of 100×10 mm tongued and grooved and V-jointed softwood. Glue together and finish to 425 mm × 300 mm

Radius to 25 mm

Radius all edges with a plane and sandpaper

Pin and glue the back panel to the sides and shelves from behind

Radius to 25 mm

Shelves from 409 mm lengths of 100×10 mm tongued and grooved and V-jointed softwood. Remove the tongue and finish the edge to a radius

Sides from 275 mm lengths of 125×19 mm planed all round softwood

Hook support from a 393 mm length of 100×10 mm of tongued and grooved and V-jointed softwood cut down to 30 mm. Pin and glue beneath shelf, then add four brass cuphooks

Miniature shelf

Finish: Sand all edges and surfaces smooth. Seal thoroughly with at least two coats of polyurethane or melamine lacquer

8
8
A

Cut grooves for the shelves with a router or tenon saw and 8 mm chisel. The slots are 90 mm long, dimensions as shown

40

40

Project

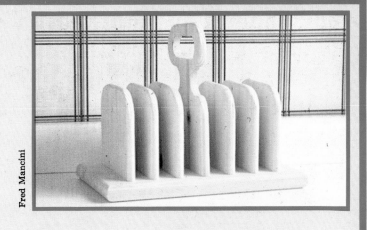
Cutting list (toast rack)

All sizes are in millimetres. Timber is planed all round (PAR) or tongued-and-grooved and V-jointed (T+G+V).

Part	Material	No.	Size
base	125mm×19mm softwood (PAR)	1	200mm
dividers	100mm×10mm softwood (T+G+V)	6	80mm
handle	100mm×10mm softwood (T+G+V)	1	143mm

Additional materials: Panel pins, PVA woodworking adhesive

Finish: Polyurethane or melamine lacquer

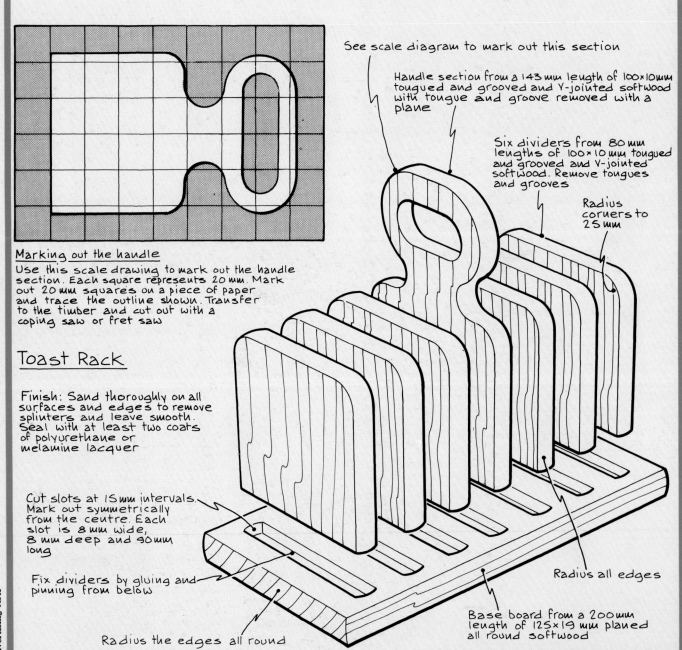

Marking out the handle

Use this scale drawing to mark out the handle section. Each square represents 20 mm. Mark out 20 mm squares on a piece of paper and trace the outline shown. Transfer to the timber and cut out with a coping saw or fret saw

Toast Rack

Finish: Sand thoroughly on all surfaces and edges to remove splinters and leave smooth. Seal with at least two coats of polyurethane or melamine lacquer

Cut slots at 15mm intervals. Mark out symmetrically from the centre. Each slot is 8 mm wide, 8 mm deep and 90mm long

Fix dividers by gluing and pinning from below

Radius the edges all round

See scale diagram to mark out this section

Handle section from a 143 mm length of 100×10mm tongued and grooved and V-jointed softwood with tongue and groove removed with a plane

Six dividers from 80 mm lengths of 100×10 mm tongued and grooved and V-jointed softwood. Remove tongues and grooves

Radius corners to 25 mm

Radius all edges

Base board from a 200mm length of 125×19 mm planed all round softwood